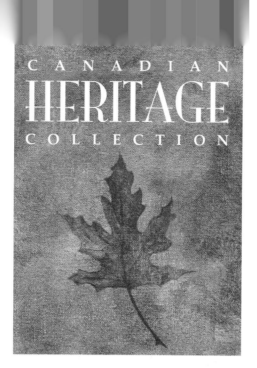

CANADIAN
HERITAGE
COLLECTION

VISUAL ART

Heather Miller

Series Editor
Don Kendal

Ru bicon

To Scott, Brett and Heidi who inspire me
and my parents Carol and Bruce Amson who encourage and support me

HEATHER MILLER

 Ru'bicon © 2003 Rubicon Education Inc.

Editorial Coordinator: Martine Quibell
Design/Production: Jennifer Drew

National Library of Canada Cataloguing in Publication

Miller, Heather
        The visual arts / Heather Miller.

(Canadian heritage collection)
Includes bibliographical references and index.
ISBN 0-921156-87-1

        1. Art—Canada. 2. Performing arts—Canada. I. Title.
II. Series: Canadian heritage collection (Oakville, Ont.)

N6545.M54 2002   700'.971   C2002-902011-5

Printed in Canada

COVER:
WILLIAM RONALD
Pierre Elliott Trudeau: Prime Ministers Series, c.1977-81,
oil and spray paint on canvas, 304.8 x 102.9 cm
Collection of the Kitchener-Waterloo Art Gallery. Gift of Mr Irving Zucker 1993

Table of Contents

INTRODUCTION

CANADIANS CELEBRATED the beginning of the 20th century filled with optimism. Life had already improved considerably during the preceding century. People had no reason to doubt Prime Minister Sir Wilfrid Laurier when he claimed that the 20th century would belong to Canada. Although cities like Winnipeg had blossomed in the late 1880s, Canada was still mainly a vast, empty wilderness — a developing country composed of four geographic regions and seven provinces. The majority of Canadians lived on farms, in lumber camps, or mining villages. They were largely ignorant of the outside world.

The wave of immigration that hit Canada in the first decade of the 20th century kept the focus on British, French, and European cultural trends. In 1902, Clifford Sifton, Minister of the Interior, launched a massive advertising program to entice farmers and farm labourers to the prairies. In less than ten years over 800 000 immigrants had settled in Canada. This marked the beginning of multiculturalism, and, coupled with the proximity of America, helped to shape how Canadian art evolved.

At the beginning of the 20th century, Canadians had developed a taste for dark, moody pictures. In Montreal, expensive Dutch paintings were especially admired by the wealthy. Those of more modest means bought cheaper versions of the same thing. The scene was similar in Toronto, where people were influenced by Montreal's elite. For example, Mary Ellen Dignam, Head of the Canadian Women's Art Association, worked tirelessly to improve public taste by promoting dark, figurative paintings. The general public, therefore, was not prepared for the direction art would take as the century unfolded.

Traditionally, Canadian artists created works according to what their patrons liked. Often artists felt like paid servants who had little freedom to experiment with their own ideas. However, by the turn of the 20th century it became easier for Canadians to study art in Europe or the United States. This greatly influenced some Canadian artists and they began to question the idea of the artist as subservient craftsperson.

The American painter James McNeill Whistler was notable in influencing the direction of Canadian art. He believed in aestheticism, an idea sometimes known as "art for art's sake." This philosophy argues that works of art have value in and of themselves based on their formal, aesthetic qualities. According to this philosophy, works should be appreciated for their own sake without taking into account reference to anything outside the work itself. This idea led to the growth of art that was driven by the artist's personal vision. Artists in America and Europe were in control of their art. Canadians like James Wilson Morrice, John Lyman, David Milne, and Lawren Harris — people who would shape the work we think of as Canadian Art — soon began to follow their lead.

Great Britain's declaration of war on Germany in 1914 brought with it an unexpected boost to the development of Canadian art. By mid-October of that year the first contingent of Canadian soldiers had landed in England. They were under the command of British generals and wore British uniforms. Sir Max Aitken (later Lord Beaverbrook) was a devoted Canadian nationalist who wanted to highlight Canadian achievements during the war. In 1916, he established the War Memorials Committee. It was responsible for commissioning artists to record Canadian participation in the war. The artists created 850 works that formed the Canadian War Memorials Collection.

World War I had a profound effect on Canadians. By the time it was over there was a growing self-confidence among the general public. By 1919 women in most of Canada had been given the vote (except in Quebec, where they had to wait until 1940). Recognized as a founding member of the League of Nations, Canada had grown in international stature and was on the path to becoming an independent nation. The optimism felt by people following the war was reflected in the art. In 1920 the Group of Seven was formed in Toronto. The members of the group were intensely nationalistic and believed that a country's art had to flourish before the country itself could grow. Their goal was to create a uniquely Canadian art that captured the spirit of the country. The Group of Seven marked the beginning of a national art movement in Canada. Their vision of Canada's raw beauty dominated landscape painting in central Canada for several decades.

The Great Depression of the 1930s made art an unnecessary luxury for most people. Many established artists became teachers to earn a living. Younger artists found it impossible to live by their art. They were also hindered by the overwhelming success of the Group of Seven's Canadianism. The style had become so completely accepted that most young artists were reluctant to try anything new. Still, innovative artists such as Carl Schaefer, Jack Humphrey, Pegi Nicol MacLeod, and Goodridge Roberts continued to explore new ideas. The hard times brought about by the Depression prompted some artists to examine social and political issues. Gradually, the organization of key art groups like the Canadian Group of Painters and the Contemporary Arts Society unified members and contributed to the growing understanding of Canadian art. These groups provided a place for artists to experiment and show their work.

In 1939, when France and Britain declared war on Germany, the Dominion of Canada joined them as an independent country. By 1943 it was apparent that the war was not going to end quickly. Once again the Official War Artists program was instituted. This time one woman, Molly Lamb Bobak, was included among the front line war artists. At home, artists created works that reflected how the war was changing life and society. War artists were somewhat conservative in their interpretation of what they saw. For the most part realism was the preferred style. It wasn't until the late 1940s that Canadian art embraced a totally new look.

The 1950s were exciting years for Canadians. Finally Sir Wilfrid Laurier's promise seemed to be coming true. Newfoundland had joined Canada in 1949. The booming economy and swelling optimism resulted in a rapid increase in the population. Canadians were justifiably proud of their growing nation. Although their optimism was tempered somewhat by the Cold War and the possibility of a nuclear attack, Canadians embraced the decade. Advances in production and marketing made all kinds of gadgets available. Television finally became affordable for the average person. To counter the American domination of the airwaves, the Canadian Broadcasting Corporation (CBC) began television broadcasting in 1952. The government was eager to preserve Canadian culture by funding Canadian programming. In 1957, the Canada Council for the Arts was founded. Its purpose was to "to foster and promote the study and enjoyment of, and the production of works in, the arts." Art was no longer an unnecessary luxury.

As Canadians became more worldly their ideas about life and art began to shift. Artists throughout Canada were pushing for change. For example, in Quebec a "Quiet Revolution" was taking hold. In 1948 Paul-Émile Borduas and fifteen other activists, mostly painters, signed the *Refus Global* (Total Refusal). In it they challenged the authority of the Catholic Church and called for radical social change and artistic freedom. Artists in much of Canada embraced Abstract Expressionism — a style that seemed to set them free. They rejected earlier ideas of national expression and turned to personal expression. Influenced by what was happening in America and Europe, artists like William Ronald in Toronto created bold, exciting images. In the early 1960s Ronald

became the host of a TV show called *The Umbrella*. Here he was able to talk about Abstract Expressionism in a way the average person could understand. Canadians were becoming more informed about the world of art.

By 1971, for the first time in history, Canadians earned about the same as their American neighbours. At the same time, almost two-thirds of Canadians (13.75 million out of 21.5 million) were under the age of thirty. They could afford to express themselves. Youth culture exploded across the country. Art markets grew and artists took on star status. More and more Canadians looked to the international scene for inspiration. Novelty and experimentation drove much of Canadian art in the decades that followed. At the same time, representational artists across Canada produced art that seemed distinctly Canadian. During the 1970s and 1980s First Nation and Inuit art gained increased recognition within the general public. This reflected the feelings of most Canadians that aboriginal peoples had been unfairly treated. Issues of aboriginal rights were in the public eye. Artists like Jane Ash Poitras and Gerald McMaster created works that dealt with these issues.

Canadians continued to embrace change throughout the 1980s and 90s. Perhaps the most significant change was the patriation of the Constitution, especially the inclusion of the Charter of Rights and Freedoms in 1982. For the first time, ordinary citizens had the ability to change the law. Another dramatic change for Canadians was the recession that gripped the country in 1990. Canada had been practically immune to major economic difficulties since 1940. People were not prepared for the fall of the Gross Domestic Product and the rise of unemployment. Tensions began to grow. Relations with Canada's aboriginal peoples were changing too. In 1990 a confrontation at Oka, Quebec pitted Mohawks against the Canadian army. For 78 days there was a highly televised standoff. Although it ended peacefully, the sense of grievance felt by the native community led to a Royal Commission on Aboriginal Peoples. In Quebec separatism became the driving force in Canadian politics. The referendum in 1995 saw a slim margin of 50.6 to 49.4 percent of Quebecers vote to stay in Canada. Throughout the final decades of the 20th century issues of race, gender, sexuality, identity, and place became the focus of artists as they struggled to make sense of their rapidly changing world. As artist Aba Bayefsky said, "Art and social comment go hand in hand."

By the end of the 1990s the economy blossomed, unemployment and inflation dropped, and Canadians flourished. Compared to the state of the arts at the beginning of the twentieth century, it could be said that the arts in Canada at the end of the century were flourishing as well.

Heather Miller

1900 - 1909

*I*n 1900 Toronto and Montreal, Canada's largest cities, were the centres for art in the country. Interest in the arts had grown with the cities, prompting artists and people in business to work together to establish art museums. The Art Association of Montreal was founded in 1860 — the first endeavour of its kind in Canada. The Art Museum of Toronto was incorporated by the Ontario Legislature in 1900. Although many Canadian artists clung to the past, others looked overseas for inspiration. For them Paris and London beckoned.

"Tonalism" is a term that describes the art being created by innovative French and British painters as the 20th century began. Tonalism was used most often to describe peaceful and dreamlike landscape paintings characterized by gentle light and faintly outlined objects. The technique was denounced by some critics, like J.A. Radford, but progressive Canadian artists supported it. In 1907, Edmund Morris and a group of like-minded Tonalist painters, along with critics and business people, formed the Canadian Art Club. Most of the members had studied in France. Artists James Wilson Morrice, Franklin Bownell, Archibald Browne, Horatio Walker, and Homer Watson were producing art that was very different from what people in Canada were used to seeing. The Canadian Art Club was formed as a way for them to exhibit their work in Canada for the first time. However, as time passed, the expense of shipping and lack of understanding of their works led members to doubt the whole idea. When Edmund Morris, the group's leader, drowned in a tragic accident in 1913, the group lost its driving force. It disbanded in 1915.

The formation of the Canadian Art Club marked the first time a group of Canadians joined together to promote artistic change and bring new concepts to Canada. Some of the later members, like William Clapp and Marc-Aurèle Suzor-Coté, continued to expand their ideas. They joined as Tonalists and were Impressionists by the time they showed their work with the Club. Liberated by the influence of Impressionism, with its loose brush strokes and atmospheric effects, they set the stage for the advance of modernism in Canada.

▲ FLORENCE CARLYLE *The Tiff*, c.1902, oil on canvas, 183.8 X 134.6 cm
Art Gallery of Ontario. Gift of the Government of the Provinces of Ontario, 1972

▼ Cartoon *The Globe*, Toronto, 16 September 1905

IN THE PICTURE GALLERY OF THE EARLS OF LONGLINE
Sir Peter Stodgely: Curious thing your family should all be took in fancy dress! I s'pose they're all by the same man eh? — Punch.

6

1902	1902	1903	1904
Winnipeg Art Society formed	American Alfred Stieglitz promotes pictorialism at his Photo-Secession in N.Y. – influences Canadian photographers	Vancouver Photographic Society formed	The Canadian Society of Graphic Arts is founded

1900
–
1909

◄ HORATIO WALKER *Ave Maria*, 1906
oil on canvas, 46 x 34 in
Art Gallery of Hamilton. Gift of the Women's Committee, 1963

▲ MAURICE CULLEN
Cape Diamond, 1909
oil on canvas, 57 x 68.5 in
Art Gallery of Hamilton. Bequest of H.L. Rinn, 1955

Somewhere during the last ten years the movement, known as 'impressionism,' first showed itself here. Though adversely criticized and spoken of as a 'craze' or 'fad,' it was something of far more importance. While we read of these wild vagaries abroad our home painters kept on in the good old way... with no distracting or startling note. Then came one and another of these canvases from abroad, or from those who had been — vague, hazy and unreal, they appeared to some, while to others they seemed visions of light and air, of sunshine and out-of-doors. Those violet shadows and crude greens were certainly peculiar, the streaks and blobs of raw colour difficult to understand. It was all very bewildering and the wise shook their heads. But by and by the most knowing were aware that in these canvases there was no attempt to paint things as they are, but as they appear, and that, in spite of its exaggerations and eccentricities, the plein-air work held a truth and had come to stay.

— M.L. Fairburn, "A Decade of Canadian Art," *Canadian Magazine*, 17 June 1901

It is sunshine, caught and absorbed: the concentrated essence of sunlight distilled through the innumerable slender tubes of wheat stalks and stored in the capsules of myriads of wheat ears....the band of wheaten gold widens and lengthens until it loses itself in the wavering uncertain horizon when the sky is no more blue, merges into a vague, unnamable, unpaintable clarity of light and air.

— C.W. Jefferys, "Trip to Saskatchewan," undated [1910] ms., Jefferys Papers, Manuscript Division, NAC, Ottawa

CHARLES WILLIAM JEFFERYS *Wheat Stacks on the Prairies,* 1907 ▲
oil on canvas, 61.9 x 91.4 cm
Government of Ontario Art Collection. Photo: Thomas Moore Photography

▼ JAMES WILSON MORRICE *The Ferry, Quebec,* 1907,
oil on canvas, 62.0 x 81.7 cm
National Gallery of Canada, Ottawa

◄ EDMUND M. MORRIS *Wolf Collar – Makoyo Ki Nasi, Medicine Man,*
1909, oil pastel on paper, 63.9 x 50 cm
Portrait Collection of the Government of Alberta. Reprinted by permission of the Speaker of the Legislative Assembly of Alberta

I am becoming doubtful about the advisability of sending pictures to Toronto. Nothing is sold (except to our friend McTavish) — nobody understands them — and it involves great expense. I have not the desire to improve the taste of the Canadian public.

— James Morrice, writing to Edmund Morris, 5 April 1908

1900
–
1909

"The time is now when there is a general movement, a reaching out for something other than mere thoughts of money and money getting. People, to live truly and nobly, require the stimulus of beauty around them…so that…while we wish for material prosperity, we may not become altogether sordid in attaining that end…"

— D.R. Wilkie, excerpt from speech made at the opening of the first Canadian Art Club exhibition, 4 February 1908

▲ CLARENCE GAGNON
Brise d'été a Dinard (Summer Breeze at Dinard)
1907, oil on canvas, 54 x 81 cm
Collection Musée du Québec, 37.01. Photo: Jean-Guy Kérouac

▶ CLARENCE GAGNON
Mont Sainte-Michel, 1907,
etching on paper
The Montreal Museum of Fine Arts

▼ WILLIAM HENRY CLAPP *In the Orchard, Québec*
1909, oil on canvas, 73.5 x 91.5 cm
Art Gallery of Hamilton. Gift of W.R. Watson, 1956

1910 - 1919

1910
James Wilson Morrice sees Manet and the Post-Impressionist exhibition in England

1911-12
Morrice makes first trip to Morocco with Henri Matisse

1912
Wassily Kandinski publishes *Concerning the Spiritual in Art*

*B*y 1910 Impressionism was generally accepted in Canada. It was being praised, in particular, in the works of Maurice Cullen who had demonstrated the ability to combine Impressionism and the Canadian spirit. Something new was on the horizon, however. Post-Impressionism was being decried by Canadian critics. The style, which placed a renewed emphasis on colour and stylization, played a defining role in the development of Canadian art. It was introduced primarily by James Wilson Morrice, John Lyman, David Milne, and Lawren Harris. These men were responsible for bringing modernism — the desire to expand the expressive possibilities of art — to Canada. Although the "new art" was strongly criticized by some, it brought renewed energy to the Canadian art scene, and inspired artists like A.Y. Jackson and Tom Thomson. Thomson painted the power of Canada's north, sparking an enduring interest in the natural environment. His work inspired other Canadian painters to explore colour harmonies and self-expression.

When Canada entered World War I in 1914, it was as a British colony, not an independent ally. However, as the war progressed, the bravery and skill shown by Canadian soldiers, along with the constant supply of manpower and munitions, made the Canadian war effort indispensable to the British. Canadian officials wanted a way to publicize the growing stature of Canada. In 1916, the Canadian War Records Office was established, with Sir Max Aitken (later Lord Beaverbrook), heading it. Seeking a way to permanently record Canada's participation in the war, he hired Canadian artists to paint both on the home front and at the front lines (male artists only). The Official War Artists were Canadians who became part of a tradition dating back to the beginning of recorded history.

Canada's war art program was larger than that of any other country. It marked the first official, large commission for Canadian artists, and included both established painters like Maurice Cullen and emerging artists like David Milne. Some of Canada's finest, best known artists, including four who would later become part of the Group of Seven, are represented in the resulting collection of works.

◀ CHARLIE JAMES
Kwakwaka'wakw Transformation Mask, c.1910, (fairly recently attributed to Charlie James by Peter Macnair, former curator of Ethnology, RBCM), red cedar, leather, paint and nails, 75 x 67 x 35 cm
Collection of Royal British Columbia Museum. RBCM Catalogue # 1908

▾ WILLIAM BRYMNER
The Vaughan Sisters, 1910, oil on canvas, 103 x 127.8 cm. Art Gallery of Hamilton. Gift of Mrs H.H. Leather, 1962

▴ MARC-AURÈLE DE FOY SUZOR-COTÉ
Les Fumées, port de Montréal, 1914 oil on canvas, 99 x 131.4 cm
Collection Musée du Québec, Photo: Patrick Altman

1913	1913	1913	1914
The National Gallery of Canada Act passed	John Lyman and A.Y. Jackson exhibit work at the Art Association of Montreal	The work of David Milne and Henri Matisse shown at the Armoury Show, New York	Art Museum of Toronto makes facilities available to Toronto Camera Club, suggesting recognition of photography as art form

1910
—
1919

▲ HELEN GALLOWAY McNICOLL
In the Shadow of the Tree, c.1914,
oil on canvas, 100.4 X 82.6 cm
Collection of the Musée du Québec. Photo: Patrick Altman

▲ J.W. BEATTY *Albain-St. Nazaire*, 1918, oil on canvas
Collection: Canadian War Museum CWM 8102

…The death of Helen McNicoll, one of the most profoundly original and technically accomplished of Canadian artists, is a matter for the sincerest regret among all lovers of art. It is now five or six years since she established herself as a personality in the Canadian field, but she has been continuously developing her powers…in which respect she afforded a striking contrast to the prevailing type of feminine painter. Possessed of an aggressive and active intellect, she was constantly applying herself to new problems of light, line and beauty, and none who saw her recent works can doubt that had she been spared she would have added materially to her own laurels and the reputation abroad of Canadian art.

— *Saturday Night*, 10 July 1915

▾ TOM THOMSON *Northern River*, 1915,
oil on canvas, 115.1 x 102 cm
National Gallery of Canada, Ottawa. Purchased 1915

TORONTO ARTIST DROWNS IN NORTH:
Body of Tom Thomson Found in Canoe Lake, Algonquin Park

The mystery surrounding the disappearance of Mr. Tom Thomson, the Toronto artist, at Canoe Lake, Algonquin Park, on Sunday, July 8, was solved yesterday by the finding of his body. Word which reached the city last night indicated that he had been drowned. His canoe was found adrift a few hours after Mr. Thomson was last seen, and the fate of the artist was a mystery until yesterday's gruesome discovery. His brother, Mr. George Thomson of New Haven, Conn., also a painter, who had been visiting the family home in Owen Sound last week when the news first came, went to the scene and joined for a time in the search. The body, it was stated, in last night's telegrams, will be buried in Algonquin Park, which had been the artist's happy sketching ground for years.

— *The Globe*, 18 July 1917

11

1914	**1914**	**1914**	**1916**
Dr. James MacCallum and Lawren Harris build the *Studio Building* in Toronto	Clive Bell (British philosopher and art critic) publishes *Art*	The National Gallery of Canada purchases *The Red Maple*, by A.Y. Jackson	Canadian War Memorials (Official War Artists) program is founded by Canadian government

"I can't get it!"

▲ *The Toronto Daily Star*, 12 December 1913

▲ A.Y. JACKSON *Houses of Ypres*, 1917, oil on linen, 63.4 x 76.1 cm
Collection: Canadian War Museum CWM 8207

Whenever we see a fresh mass of color on the club walls, with an accompanying diagram in black and white showing what each splash costs, if it is not marked down before next Friday, we know that another Exhibition of Paintings by a distinguished Centre Forward of the Hot Mush School is afoot and that we must have care.

— H.F. Gadsby, "The Hot Mush School or Peter and I," *The Toronto Daily News*, 12 December 1913

It can be demonstrated that every one of these pictures is sound in composition. Their colour is good, in some cases superbly good; not one of them is too large. Their nationality is unmistakable. Undoubtedly they are not what the artist would like them to be, but they are truly interpretive if one understands and is interested in the Canadian landscape...in a new country like ours which is practically unexplored artistically, courageous experiment is not only legitimate but vital to the development of living Canadian art. [The painters]...are but striving to enlarge their own conception of that spirit. And they remember sometimes that the best in this kind are but shadows and the worst are no worse, if imagination amend them.

— J.E.H. MacDonald, letter to the editor, "Bouquets from a Tangled Garden," *The Globe*, 27 March 1916

▶ JAMES EDWARD HERVEY (J.E.H.) MACDONALD *The Tangled Garden*, 1916, oil on beaverboard, 121.4 x 152.4 cm
National Gallery of Canada, Gift of W.M. Southam, F.N. Southam and H.S. Southam, 1937, in memory of their brother Richard Southam

1916	1916	1917	1918
Canadian Society of Painters-Etchers and Engravers founded	Parliament Buildings in Ottawa destroyed by fire	Conscription in Canada; Tom Thomson drowns	Women in Canada, except Quebec, given the vote

1910
—
1919

▲ MARGARET WATKINS *The Kitchen Sink*, c.1919,
palladium print, 21.3 x 16.4 cm National Gallery of Canada, Ottawa.
Purchased 1984 with the assistance of a grant from the Govt. of Canada under the
terms of the Cultural Property Export and Import Act

▲ LOUIS-PHILIPPE HÉBERT
Algonquins, 1916, bronze, 67.0 x 65.4 x 22.4 cm
Collection de la Musée du Québec. Photo: Patrick Altman

▲ OZIAS LEDUC *Neige Dorée (Guilded
Snow)*, 1916, oil on canvas, 137.8 x 77.2 cm
National Gallery of Canada, Ottawa. Purchased 1916

The distinguished painter, Mr. J. W. Morrice, sends from Paris several of his most characteristic works. They all have that peculiar poetry — that tranquillity of feeling — which makes them pictures you would want to live with, whose message is not conveyed at a single glimpse — pictures that are subtle and persuasive in their appeal…

A painter whose work is far less familiar to art lovers in this part of Canada than it should be, is Mr. A. Suzor-Coté of Montreal. In truth his work is so individual, so genuinely Canadian for the most part, as to delight all who aspire toward a national art.

— Hector Charlesworth "The Canadian Art Club," *Saturday Night,* 24 May 1913

Visitors will see on the walls little departure from the so well beaten track — the hall-mark of modernism is upon nearly all of the pictures. Remarkably few depict scenes and incidents that are purely Canadian. With few exceptions the contributors are London and Paris trained.

— Review in the *Manchester Guardian* of The Exhibitions – Fourth Decade (Referring to 113 pictures and 5 bronzes sent to England in June 1910 for exhibition at the Festival of Empire at the Crystal Palace); in the *History of the Royal Canadian Academy of the Arts,* Hugh G. Jones and Edmund Dyonnet, 1934

13

1920 - 1929

1920
Group of Seven founded in Toronto –
hold their first exhibition at the Art
Museum of Toronto

1920
The Art Museum of Toronto becomes
the Art Museum of Ontario

In the years following World War I, Canada was gripped by a wave of nationalism. Canadians felt they had "grown up." They were Canadians, not colonials, and they were looking for distinctive Canadian symbols. This sense of nationalism was especially strong among a group of men who, along with Tom Thomson, had been exploring Canada's north and painting together for years. These artists were good friends. Several of them worked together at Grip Limited, a commercial design company. They had banded together because of their common vision and the outrage of Canadian art critics towards their work. Their name, the Group of Seven, was first used in 1920 for a large show that was held at the Toronto Art Museum. Inspired by Tom Thomson, the members of the group (Lawren Harris, A.Y. Jackson, Fred Varley, Frank Johnston, Arthur Lismer, Franklin Carmichael, and J.E.H. MacDonald) wanted to paint Canada in a way that captured the spirit of the country. They experienced the height of their cohesiveness as a group from about 1914 to the early 1920s. By the mid 1920s, with their work increasingly accepted by mainstream Canadians, many of the members began to grow in different directions and their focus became more personal. The Group of Seven introduced Canadianism and an entirely new style of landscape painting — one that, for many people, has come to symbolize Canada.

While the Group of Seven was breaking new ground in Central Canada, Emily Carr was working in virtual isolation in British Columbia. Like the Group of Seven, she suffered the ridicule of local citizens and critics. In 1912 she painted almost 200 works representing more than 15 native villages along the coast of British Columbia. It wasn't until 1927, however, that 26 of those paintings were exhibited, in the National Museum of Canada's Exhibition of West Coast Art — Native and Modern. This was an important turning point for Carr. She met members of the Group of Seven and finally felt that she was not alone. Emily Carr captured the spirit of the Natives and the land in a uniquely Canadian way. As a result, she is one of Canada's most famous female painters.

In Montreal the influence of Post-Impressionism was felt by a group of artists who formed the Beaver Hall Hill Group. These 19 artists, many of them women, met and exhibited their work from 1920-22.

GROUP OF SEVEN

▲ Photo: The Group of Seven, Luncheon at the Arts & Letters Club, Toronto, c.1920: From Left: Varley, Jackson, Harris, Barker, Fairley (non-member), Johnston, Lismer, MacDonald, gelatin silver print on paper, 9.0 x 12.2 cm
Art Gallery of Ontario. Purchase Corporations' Subscription Endowment, 1966

First Exhibition Catalogue ▲
Exhibition of Paintings,
7-27 May 1920
Art Museum of Toronto, The Edward P. Taylor Research Library and Archives, Art Gallery of Ontario

There has been a great deal of talk of late in England and elsewhere about "representative Canadian art," especially in connection with a group of Toronto painters who hold that Canada is only truly interpreted through a single narrow and rigid formula of ugliness. Many Canadians of taste and discrimination who went abroad to visit the British Empire Exhibition…have lately returned, and expressions of disgust are to be heard on all sides at the unrepresentative character of what the London critics have been led to believe is "representative" Canadian art. … the cult of ugliness is so glaringly and insistently exemplified on the walls of the Canadian gallery that canvases of this order overshadow and "kill" pictures of a truly thoughtful and interpretative character.

— Frederick Paul, Editor, *Saturday Night,* 8 November 1924

▲ LAWREN HARRIS *Elevator Court, Halifax,* 1921,
oil on canvas, 96.5 x 112.1 cm
Art Gallery of Ontario. Gift from the Albert H. Robson Memorial Subscription Fund, 1941

Arthur Lismer

▲ ARTHUR LISMER *The Explorers and Builders of Canada*, 1927-32
Reproduced with permission of the Learnxs Foundation. Photo: Tom Moore

The Lismer Mural in Lismer Hall, Humberside Collegiate Institute, Toronto, tells the story of Canadian values, exploration, and settlement.

February 19th, 1927

A scheme for the decoration of the west wall in the auditorium of Humberside Collegiate Institute has been arranged and this is a statement of the agreement between Humberside Collegiate Institute and Arthur Lismer who will undertake the work.

The scheme provides for five panels to be completed as the funds of the Literary Society of the Collegiate Institute permit. The completion of the first panel is definitely arranged for and subsequent panels are to be done over a period of three or four years. The sketches and plans for the completed wall shall be the property of the Collegiate Institute and the first, or central, panel is to be commenced forthwith and the costs of this is agreed upon to be not more than FOUR HUNDRED DOLLARS.

(Signed) Arthur Lismer
(Signed) S.B. Hatch, Chairman of the Committee for School
(Signed) Ada L. Ward, Secretary of Committee for School

"Humberside Collegiate Institute of Toronto and its students have a long tradition, stretching back to 1926, of sponsoring Canadian artists. Arthur Lismer was commissioned to paint what is thought to be the largest Canadian mural — The Humberside Lismer Mural. This famous painting was dismantled, damaged and partially lost during school reconstruction. Mel Greif [Head of History Department] raised over $100000.00 from alumni and government and cultural sources and arranged for the repatriation and de-accessioning of the missing pieces. He hired conservators from Queen's University. After 15 years of creative and hard work, the glorious mural once again hangs in its full majesty in the school auditorium, renamed Lismer Hall."

— Speech at presentation of Jane Jacobs Award 2002 (Ideas that Matter), to Mel Greif, at Arts and Letters Club, Toronto

"[the painter of murals] must possess a different mental and spiritual equipment, a sense of orchestration and a powerful imagination…a nature that can rise above the objective and literal, and the ability to sacrifice mere personal caprice in the service of a bigger thing than himself. The ability to think, to visualize noble proportions, to project onto the surface of the wall a nobler, grander pattern of life than the fussy realism of the average subject picture is a prime essential in art."

— Arthur Lismer, article in *Journal of the Royal Architectural Institute of Canada*, July 1933

▲ ARTHUR LISMER *Johnston, Carmichael and Varley*, 1920, charcoal on paper, 25.4 x 20.2 cm
Art Gallery of Ontario. Gift of Mrs R.M. Tovell 1983, transferred from the Edward P. Taylor Reference Library

1925	1925	1926	1926
The Canadian Society of Painters in Watercolour is founded	The first major history of Canadian art, *The Fine Arts in Canada* published	*The Story of the Group of Seven* by F.B Housser, the first book about a Canadian art movement, published	Art Students League of Toronto founded

▸ ANNE SAVAGE *La Maison Rouge (The Red House), Dorval,* c.1928, oil on canvas, 51 x 61.7 cm
Collection: Musée de Québec. Photo: Jean-Guy Kérouac

When ever I could afford it I went up north among the Indians and the woods and forgot all about everything in the joy of those lonely wonderful places, I decided to try to make as good a representative collection of those old villages and wonderful totem poles as I could, for the love of the people, and the love of the places, and the love of the art, whether anybody liked them or not I did not care a bean.

— Emily Carr, *Autobiography for Eric Brown* (Director National Gallery of Canada), 1 November 1927

◂ ELIZABETH WYN WOOD *Northern Island,* 1927, cast tin on black glass base,
20.5 x 37.7 x 20.8 cm; base 2 x 71 x 40.5 cm
National Gallery of Canada, Ottawa. Bequest of Mrs J.P. Barwick (from the Douglas M. Duncan Collection) 1985

"Canada reveals herself in colours all her own, colours in which the environment of Nature plays no insignificant part. She has mixed her colours with her restless unrestrained energy, her uncontrolled forces. We feel, as we look at these pictures, the rush of the mighty winds as they sweep the prairies, the swirl and roar of the swollen river torrents, and the awful silent majesty of her snows. And such is Canada's art — the "pourings out" of men and women whose souls reflect the expansiveness of their wide horizons, who dream their dreams, "and express themselves in form and colour" upon the canvas."

— J.M. Millman, Overseas press comments on the Canadian Section of Fine Arts, British Empire Exhibition, 1924-25

◂ THOMAS FRIPP *Glacier on D'Arcy Range,* 1924 watercolour on paper, 39.0 x 49.7 cm,
Vancouver Art Gallery, VAG 40.11. Photo: Teresa Healy

1927
Emily Carr's work is included in a show of Canadian West Coast Art, Native and Modern, at the National Museum of Canada in Ottawa

1927
Toronto hosts International Exhibition of Modern Art from the Société Anonyme, New York

1928
Sculptors' Society of Canada founded in Toronto

1929
David Milne stays in Canada; stock market crashes setting off Great Depression

▲ EMILY COONAN *Girl in Dotted Dress*, c.1923, oil on canvas, 76 x 66.4 cm
Art Gallery of Hamilton. Gift of *The Spectator* 1968

▲ A.J. CASSON *Saturday Afternoon*, c.1927, watercolour over graphite on paper, 46.9 x 62.3 cm
McMichael Canadian Art Collection. Gift of Mr. & Mrs. C.A.G. Matthews (1974.13.2)

▼ BERTRAM BROOKER *Sounds Assembling*, 1928, oil on canvas, 112.3 x 91.7 cm
Collection of the Winnipeg Art Gallery (#L-80)

Of the members of the Group of Seven…only Frank Carmichael, myself and Fred Varley did serious watercolour painting…the emphasis of the Group was squarely on oils. Collectors were not interested in watercolour; they wanted to feel and smell the oil on the canvas.

The inferior status of watercolours was reflected in exhibitions, where they would normally be hung in corridors or in the furthest, darkest reaches of the exhibition hall.

I came to the conclusion that in order to secure a place of respect for watercolours an official society of watercolour painters would have to be formed.

— A.J. Casson, *My Favourite Watercolours, 1919 to 1957*

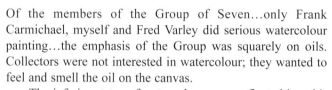

▲ Installation, *Exhibition of Canadian West Coast Art – Native and Modern* (featuring three of Emily Carr's works), 1927
National Gallery of Canada, Ottawa. NGC Library and Archives

1930 - 1939

1930
Lawren Harris and A.Y. Jackson
go to the Arctic to paint

1932
Art Gallery of Toronto holds
last official exhibition of Group
of Seven

Canadians were particularly hard hit by the Great Depression. The economic decline coupled with nature's devastating blow to agriculture made life almost unbearable. By 1933 one out of every five people depended on government relief for survival. Many returned "to the land" rather than face the misery of trying to exist on urban relief. For the first time in 50 years, rural populations, with the exception of Saskatchewan, grew faster than urban populations. Political and social unrest throughout the decade eventually resulted in governments taking increased responsibility for social welfare.

Art sales were almost nonexistent in this difficult era. Many artists turned to teaching or commercial design to make ends meet. These were particularly frustrating times for younger artists. They couldn't sell their paintings, and had little hope of earning enough money to further their studies. On top of this, the work of the Group of Seven had become so widely accepted as the only "real" Canadian art that any new experimentation seemed pointless.

Growing controversy over the dominance of the Group of Seven resulted in it being expanded and renamed The Canadian Group of Painters in 1933. This new group included progressive English speaking artists from across Canada. In Montreal the outspoken artist John Lyman worried that Canadian art was on the brink of becoming "souvenir painting." He was responsible for the formation of the Contemporary Art Society in 1939.

This was a time when new subject matter, or a new slant on old subject matter, began to show up in Canadian art. The figure and contemporary life became the focus for artists like Paraskeva Clark, who urged her fellow painters to get involved in what was happening in their own times. Industrialization, and the progress and better life it promised, brought a renewed interest in recording Canada's industrial sites. American ideas like abstraction and regionalism began to appear in Canadian art. Many artists became intensely interested in their immediate surroundings and political and social issues. Artworks from this decade reflect the artists' responses to their rapidly changing and uncertain world.

▲ WALTER J. PHILLIPS *York Boat on Lake Winnipeg*, 1930, colour woodcut on japan paper, 29.6 x 38.7 cm
National Gallery of Canada, Ottawa. Purchased 1948

◀ Photo: Yvonne McKague Housser, 1931
National Archives of Canada

▼ YVONNE MCKAGUE HOUSSER *Cobalt*, 1931, oil on canvas, 114.8 x 140 cm
National Gallery of Canada, Ottawa. Purchased 1932

▲ LAWREN HARRIS *Mt. Lefroy*,
1930, oil on canvas, 133.5 x 153.5 cm
McMichael Canadian Art Collection (1975.7). Purchased 1975

1930
—
1939

▲ EMILY CARR *Scorned as Timber, Beloved of the Sky*,
1935, oil on canvas, 112 x 68.9 cm
Vancouver Art Gallery, VAG 42.15. Photo: Trevor Mills

[Emily Carr] who, unlike Milne, is at her best when she is working on a big scale. And her best is magnificent. If the word "genius" (a word to be jealously guarded by the critic and used only on very special occasions) can be applied to any Canadian artist it can be applied to her. She belongs to no school. Her inspiration is derived from within herself. Living among the moist mountains and giant pines of British Columbia, a country climactically different from the rest of Canada, she has had to invent a new set of conventions, a personal style of her own. Where the Eastern Canadians have been content to stylise the outward pageantry of the landscape, she has symbolised its inner meaning, and in doing so, has, as it were, humanised it. Her trees are more than trees: they are green giants, and slightly malevolent giants at that. The totem poles she often paints are haunted by the Indian deities they represent. Her art is not easy to describe, and indeed her power can hardly be felt in the four works shown in London. It happens that I saw over a hundred of her paintings when I was in Victoria. To see them was rather like reading an epic. Four short quotations cannot adequately represent the cumulative effect of the whole.

— Eric Newton, "Canadian Art Through English Eyes," *Canadian Forum*, February 1939. Emily Carr published *Klee Wyck* which won the Governor General award for Literature in 1941.

▲ PRUDENCE HEWARD *Sisters of Rural Quebec*,
1930, oil on canvas, 157.4 x 106.6 cm
Collection of the Art Gallery of Windsor. Gift of the Women's Committee, 1962

▲ WILLIAM GOODRIDGE ROBERTS *Portrait of a Lady in a Green Hat,* c.1936, oil on canvas, 53.3 x 40 cm
The Edmonton Art Gallery Collection. Purchased with funds donated by the Women's Society of the Edmonton Art Gallery

…an exhibition of paintings and drawings by John Russell was hung in the art galleries of a Toronto department store. Mr. Russell, a Canadian artist who has lived for a good many years in Paris, had contributed to the Canadian National Exhibition, a couple of years earlier, a nude which had caused a furor in the Toronto press. The puritanical Toronto public flocked to see it.

Another nude (not the same one, as so many people seemed to think) was included by Mr. Russell in the paintings sent to this store. It was hung with two or three other canvases in a tiny room off one of the main galleries, behind a closed door which no one would think of opening unless attention was called to it. The newspapers, of course, quickly apprised the public of the existence of this closeted nude, and when asked by curious visitors the store management made signs in the direction of the closed and inconspicuous door. Not a word of criticism appeared in the Toronto press regarding this bootlegging of the nude.

— Bertram Brooker "Nudes and Prudes," in *Open House*, 1931

▲ ISABEL MCLAUGHLIN *Tree*, 1935, oil on canvas, 203.5 x 92 cm
National Gallery of Canada, Ottawa. Purchased 1984

1938
Ryerson Press launches
the *Canadian Artists* series

1939
John Lyman founds
Contemporary Arts
Society in Montreal

1939
Lawren Harris becomes a member of
newly-founded Transcendental Group of
Painters in Santa Fe, New Mexico

1939
Isabel MacLaughlin becomes
first woman artist to head the
Canadian Group of Painters

▲ MARC-AURÈL FORTIN *L'Orme à Pont-Viau
(The Elm at Pont-Viau)*, c.1935, oil on canvas,
137 x 166.4 cm

Collection: Musée du Québec. Photo: Patrick Altman

▼ PARASKEVA CLARK *Petroushka*,
1937, oil on canvas, 122.4 x 81.9 cm
National Gallery of Canada, Ottawa.

▲ FRANCES LORING *Goal Keeper*, c.1935,
plaster with patina, H 242 cm
Art Gallery of Ontario. Gift of the Estates of Frances Loring
and Florence Wylie, 1983

1930
—
1939

Very few people are interested in painting aside from representation…Tom Thomson isn't popular for what aesthetic qualities he showed, but because his work is close enough to representation to get by the average man; besides his subjects were ones that have pleasant associations for most of us, holidays, rest, recreation. Pleasant associations, beautiful subject; beautiful subject, good painting. Then in Canada we like our heavens made to order and in our own image. They mustn't be too good and above all too different. The humiliating truth is that Canada's ideal is law, family, possessions, amusement, the life of a human animal, that is about it. No painting, music or literature as aesthetic experience, no quickening of life, no creative courage! Everything must contribute directly to survival or we lose interest. We borrow even this, machines, methods, inventions. It is doubtful if we can get away with it, we can't forever take and not make some effort to give.

— David Milne, letter, 1936, *Canadian Art*, Spring 1954 Vol. XI No. 3

… there has been a lot of persistent effort to establish painting which has no reflection of the Canadian background. The international outlook is the thing and from that standpoint it is of very little importance. There has at the same time been an effort to belittle the Canadian movement by people who have no feeling for the country and it has resulted in a kind of sneer when the north country is mentioned. With all the young people here there is no longer any desire to go north. They do still life and back yards and when you try to arrange an international show it is almost impossible to find a dozen canvases of any distinction.

— A.Y. Jackson in a letter to H.O. McCurry, 9 June 1938 (National Gallery of Canada)

21

1940 - 1949

1940	1941	1941
Women in Quebec get the vote	The Federation of Canadian Artists founded in Toronto	Emily Carr's book *Klee Wyck* wins Governor General's Award

War dominated the first half of the 1940s. Canada entered the war in 1939 intent on playing a much smaller role than it had during the Great War. However, as the fighting raged on and Britain became increasingly vulnerable, Canada's war effort increased. Britain and the U.S. had implemented a war artists' program at the start of the war, but it was only after considerable lobbying by artists, art societies, the National Gallery and Vincent Massey, that Prime Minister Mackenzie King sanctioned the recruitment of Canadian war artists on 19 December 1942. By the end of the war 32 names had been added to the list of Official War Artists. The first female war artist was Molly Lamb Bobak who served in northwestern Europe.

Prior to World War II, Canadians had suffered great hardships because of the Depression. The end of the war ushered in a new period of prosperity. The Gross National Product had doubled during the war, and it continued to grow. Jobs were plentiful and people could afford to buy homes and cars and start families. Canadians felt optimistic about the future in their increasingly sophisticated and complex country. In 1949 the Massey Commission was convened. It was the most thorough study of Canadian culture to date and introduced an exciting new era for the arts in Canada.

The 1940s saw Canadian art break old boundaries. Montreal became the centre of innovation. In 1940, Alfred Pellan returned after living twelve years in Paris. He brought with him great enthusiasm for Surrealism and André Bréton's ideas about "automatic writing." Pellan's art inspired young artists to work with greater freedom and creativity.

Paul-Émile Borduas was intrigued by Bréton's concept of automatic writing and began making art in a spontaneous, automatic way. He attracted a group of enthusiastic students around him and in 1947 they formed Les Automatistes. In 1948 Borduas wrote *Refus Global* (Global Refusal). It is possibly the most significant document in the history of Canadian art and a pivotal event in Quebec history. It gave voice to the dissatisfaction people felt about the restrictions to culture and life under the leadership of the Roman Catholic Church and the government of Maurice Duplessis. The scandal that *Refus Global* unleashed caused the winds of change in Canada.

▲ MILLER BRITTAIN
The Rummage Sale,
1940, oil on masonite,
63.5 x 50.9 cm
National Gallery of Canada, Ottawa

▶ Cartoon
Globe and Mail,
18 February 1943

▲ ABA BAYEFSKY *Belsen Concentration Camp — Malnutrition #2*, c.1945, charcoal, 34.9 x 41.4 cm
Collection: Canadian War Museum CWM10843

▲ CHARLES COMFORT *Dead German and the Hitler Line*, 1944, watercolour, red chalk, pencil and black ink on paper, 38.8 x 56.8 cm
Collection: Canadian War Museum CWM12272

◄ ALEX COLVILLE *Bodies in a Grave*, 1946, oil on canvas 75 x 100 cm
Collection: Canadian War Museum CWM12122

1940
–
1949

▼ LAWREN P. HARRIS *Tank Advance*, 1944, oil on linen, 75.8 x 101.2 cm
Collection: Canadian War Museum CWM12722

…Artists were commissioned to the three services, Navy, Army and Air Force, given official rank and sent to various units overseas.

As a result of the art competitions held by the Army and Air Force several young painters who had little previous recognition were brought to light and were given commissions as war artists, among them Bruno Bobak, Pat Cowley-Brown, Aba Bayefsky and Molly Lamb.

While we were late in getting started, our artists were in time to take part in the invasion of Sicily and Italy, and a great amount of first-hand material has been accumulated. Most of the work is the direct statement of the eye witness, war seen through the eyes of an individual, some coldly factual or reflecting in varying degrees how the artist feels.

— A.Y. Jackson, "A Record of Total War," *Canadian Art*, Summer 1946, Vol. III No. 4

▲ MOLLY LAMB BOBAK
Private Roy, Canadian Women's Army Corps, 1946,
oil on masonite, 76.3 x 60.7 cm
Collection: Canadian War Museum CWM12082

▲ Photo: First Official Canadian War Artists, 1946. From left: Seated, H.O. McCurry, A.Y. Jackson. Standing, O. Fisher, G. Pepper, W. Ogilve, E.J. Hughes, M.L. Bobak, C. Comfort, G.F.G. Stanley, historical officer, A. Colville, C. Tinning, B. Bobak. Behind them is *A Canadian Gun Pit* painted by Wyndham Lewis in WW I. National Gallery of Ontario, Ottawa. Photo: Courtesy NGC Library and Archives

Exhibition authorities at the Regina Fair in Canada "refused to hang a nude painting by the well-known English painter Matthew Smith," even though it was one of the works in the Massey Collection of Modern English Painting, presented to Canada by the Right Honourable Vincent Massey, and was on tour of Canada before being hung in the National Gallery of Canada.

Winnipeg Art Gallery later "condemned" the same painting on the grounds that it would offend "the respectable families" of that city.

— Louis Muhlstock, "An Excess of Prudery," *Canadian Art*, Autumn 1947, Vol. 5 No. 2

▲ JEAN-PAUL MOUSSEAU *Untitled*, 1947, ink and watercolour on paper, 22.2 x 30.2 cm
La Collection Lavalin du Musée d'art contemporain de Montréal
©SODRAC. Photo: Richard-Max Trembly

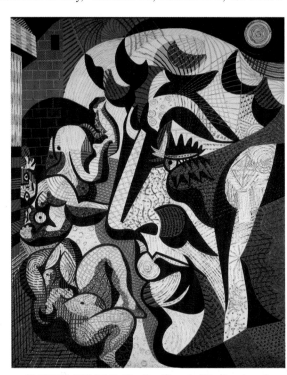

▲ ALFRED PELLAN *On the Beach (Sur la plage)*, 1945, oil on canvas, 207.7 x 167.6 cm
National Gallery of Canada, Ottawa.

24

1948	1948	1949	1949
The Contemporary Art Society disbands in Montreal	Prisme d'yeux founded in Montreal lead by Alfred Pellan	Canadian Handicrafts Guild in Montreal holds first exhibition of Inuit carvings and crafts – marks the beginning of the contemporary era of Inuit art	Saskatchewan establishes first public arts foundation in North America

▲ PAUL-ÉMILE BORDUAS *Leeward of the Island (1.47)*, 1947, oil on canvas, 114.7 x 147.7 cm
National Gallery of Canada, Ottawa. Purchased 1953

▾ B.C. BINNING *Fairweather Signals,* 1949, oil, ink, pencil on canvas, 81.5 x 103.4 cm
Vancouver Art Gallery, VAG 70.2. Photo: Teresa Healy

GLOBAL REFUSAL
Paul-Émile Borduas – August 1948

…Therefore, our duty is simple:

To break definitively with all conventions of society and its utilitarian spirit! We refuse to live knowingly at less than our spiritual and physical potential; refuse to close our eyes to the vices and confidence tricks perpetuated in the guise of learning, favour, or gratitude; refuse to be ghettoed in an ivory tower, well-fortified but too easy to ignore; refuse to remain silent — do with us what you will, but you shall hear us; refuse to make a deal with la gloire and its attendant honours: stigmata of malice, unawareness or servility; refuse to serve and to be used for such ends, refuse all intention, evil weapon of reason — down with them, to second place!

Make way for magic!
Make way for objective mysteries!
Make way for love!
Make way for necessities!

…Let those who are inspired by this endeavour join us.

We foresee a future in which man is freed from useless chains, to realize a plenitude of individual gifts, in necessary unpredictability, spontaneity and resplendent anarchy.

Until then, without surrender or rest, in community of feeling with those who thirst for better life, without fear of set-backs, in encouragement or persecution, we shall pursue in joy our overwhelming need for liberation.

— Translation by François-Marc Gagnon and Dennis Young, in Gagnon's edition, *Paul-Émile Borduas: Écrits/Writings 1942-1958*

1940
–
1949

▲ Photo: Reunion of the Automatistes during the exhibition at 75, Sherbrooke West Street, Apt. 5, February 1947. From left: Claude Gauvreau, Mrs. Gauvreau (mother), Pierre Gauvreau, Marcel Barbeau, Madeleine Arbour, Paul-Émile Borduas, Madeleine Lalonde, Bruno Cormier, Jean-Paul Mousseau
Collection: Musée d'art contemporain de Montréal, Fonds Borduas. Photo: Maurice Perron

1950 - 1959

1950
Kenneth Lochhead becomes the director of the Regina College School of Art

1950
Pop art is introduced in the U.S.

1952
CBC broadcasts Canada's first (part-time) television programs

The 1950s were a time of stability and prosperity in Canada. American influence became stronger as Canadians travelled across the border on shopping trips, and Americans flocked to the Canadian north for vacations. This was the decade when television, which had been around since the 1920s, finally became affordable. Suburbs sprang up across the nation and the great "baby boom" began. In 1957 the Canada Council, a government body, was formed to support and encourage growth of the arts.

Artists in the 1950s began to respond to the ideas they had encountered during and following World War II. Old ideas of Canadianism gave way to art as personal expression. Abstract Expressionism in Canada was a style that emphasized spontaneity and freedom. It was bold and passionate and allowed those who believed in it a way of connecting with their inner spirit. Although the 1950s offered great promise for the future, the threat of nuclear war and the growth of consumerism introduced various levels of anxiety to society. Abstract Expressionism offered an antidote for that anxiety.

William Ronald was pivotal in bringing Abstract Expressionism to Toronto. He had become a keen advocate of the style while studying in New York. Building on an American trend to show avant-garde art in department stores, Ronald arranged to have a show of abstracts at the Robert Simpson Company. "Abstracts at Home," October 1953, was trying to cultivate a more sophisticated taste for modern products. Following this show Painters Eleven was formed. The members came together to show their work and support each other. Painters Eleven played a key role in changing the nature of Canadian art.

In Montreal artists like Guido Molinari and Claude Tousignant were part of the Plasticiens, a group that followed the Automatistes in 1954. They stressed pure colour and geometric pattern in their work. Jack Shadbolt and Gordon Smith in Vancouver were among a growing number of abstract painters throughout Canada. In 1956, the National Gallery of Canada organized the first exhibition of Canadian abstract painting to travel to the U.S.. By the end of the decade abstract art was everywhere in Canada.

▲ OSCAR CAHÉN *Animated Item*, c.1955, oil on canvas, 71.5 x 87 cm
National Gallery of Canada, Ottawa. Purchased 1992

…Canadian painting, through its honesty and its artistic value, has become above all the other arts the great means of giving expression to the Canadian spirit. Canadian painting has become one of the elements of our national unity…But in order to perform his civilizing function, both within and without our country, the Canadian painter must receive appropriate encouragement. The problem facing Canadians is to find a practical means of giving the painter a place in our national life as important as the place which he himself in his art gives to the moral and material aspects of our way of living.

— "The Problems of Painters and Galleries," The Massey Commission, tabled in 1951, *Documents in Canadian Art*

▲ GERSHON ISKOWITZ *Yzkor,* 1952, watercolour and ink on paper, 31 x 41 cm
Reproduced with permission

◄ ALEX COLVILLE *Horse and Train*, 1954, glazed tempera on masonite, 41.2 x 54.2 cm
Art Gallery of Hamilton. Gift of Dominion Foundries and Steel Ltd. (DOFASCO INC.) 1957

▼ JEAN-PAUL RIOPELLE *Pavanne*, 1954, oil on canvas, 300 x 550.2 cm
National Gallery of Canada, Ottawa ©SODRAC. Purchased 1953

Jean-Paul Riopelle was a giant in our midst.

As Canada's most acclaimed painter internationally, his body of work helped to define Canadian art as it is today. With Paul-Émile Borduas, he hurtled into the mainstream of art with Les Automatistes — a group of painters from Quebec whose raw energy broke the shackles of a society they felt restricted and repressed them. Their rallying cry for freedom was the manifesto Le Refus Global (Global Refusal) in which artists were urged to "Break permanently with the customs of society, dissociate [themselves] from its utilitarian values. Refuse to live knowingly beneath the level of [their] physical potential..."

Riopelle lived his life as an artist true to those principles. His powerful and adventurous use of colour, his physical technique are matchless. His ability to fill huge canvases until the end of his life, even when he was physically not strong, attested to his mastery of the space that an artist can occupy by his profound will to create, his passionate need to innovate and his unyielding courage to persevere.

— Message from Her Excellency the Right Honourable Adrienne Clarkson, Governor General of Canada, on the death of Jean-Paul Riopelle, 13 March 2002

▲ PAUL-ÉMILE BORDUAS *L'Étoile Noire (The Black Star)*, 1957, oil on canvas, 159.4 x 128.1 cm
Montreal Museum of Fine Arts (1960.1238)

…Do I think that Global Refusal has a universal importance? No! Plagues, world wars, our giddy mechanization have this: it is on these that the fate of nations more or less depends. Notwithstanding the spiritual elements of Global Refusal, its worldly impact is nil, in spite of some French, English, Japanese and American echoes. Foreign response has been thoughtlessly to identify the text with the Surrealist line then current, without perceiving its divergent character; and Canadian criticism has not been more lucid — quite the contrary. And that is about it. A bit later, pretty well everywhere, a similar wave arose, happily disengaged from Surrealism. This wave has a universal significance, and the credit for it must go particularly to New York — which owes us nothing, of course. What remains are invisible progressions with unpredictable effects, of which nobody can speak; but of which from time to time the strangest news reaches us.

— Paul-Émile Borduas, "Global Refusal: Ten Years After," in *Documents in Canadian Art*, 1987

▲ Photo: Painters Eleven, 1957
From left: Tom Hodgson, Alexandra Luke, Harold Town, Kazuo Nakamura, Jock Macdonald, Walter Yarwood, Hortense Gordon, Jack Bush, Ray Mead.

◄ J.W.G. "JOCK" MACDONALD, *Iridescent Monarch*, 1957, oil, acrylic resin Lucite 44, and sand on hardboard, 105.7 x 121.8 cm
Art Gallery of Hamilton. Gift of the Canada Council 1960

◄ JEAN-PHILIPPE DALLAIRE
Audrey, 1957, oil on canvas,
86.2 x 66.4 cm
National Gallery of Canada, Ottawa
©SODRAC. Purchased 1958

The Canada Council for the Arts is a national arm's-length agency created by an Act of Parliament in 1957. According to the Canada Council Act, the role of the Council is "to foster and promote the study and enjoyment of, and the production of works in, the arts."

► FERNAND LEDUC *Solar Strata*,
1958, oil enamel on canvas,
160 x 113.9 cm
The Montreal Museum of Fine Arts (1995.20)
©SODRAC

1950
—
1959

▲ ARMAND VAILLANCOURT *Sculpture No. 1*,
c.1959-61, welded steel, 47 x 225 x 25 cm
National Gallery of Canada, Ottawa. Purchased 1985

▼ JEAN-PAUL LEMIEUX *L'Été (Summer)*, 1959, oil on canvas, 58.4 x 126.4 cm
Museum London (60.A110). Gift of Maclean Hunter Publishing Co. Ltd., Toronto 1960

1960
Charles Comfort becomes first artist to be director of the National Gallery of Canada

1961
The Regina Five is founded in Regina

1961
Clement Greenberg publishes *Art and Culture*

Nineteen-sixty ushered in a decade of political and social turmoil. Young people filled coffee houses, experimented with drugs, and revelled in loud music and sexual freedom. The gap between generations widened and confrontations between young and old were felt in cities across the country. This was the decade of Elvis and the Beatles, pop culture and rock.

The 1960s saw unprecedented growth in the arts stimulated by the Canada Council and the growth of commercial galleries. Artists became celebrities, art markets grew, and the world seemed to get smaller as Canadians became more aware of international issues. New York was the centre of the art world and a magnet for Canadian artists who began to enter the international scene. In 1965, for example, Guido Molinari, Claude Tousignant, Yves Gaucher, Kenneth Lochhead, Arthur McKay, and Jack Bush were all included in various New York art exhibitions.

Like everything else in Canada, art went through dramatic changes as artists reacted to art movements of the 1950s and the growing influence of media in everyday life. Post-Painterly Abstraction, a popular American style, emerged in Canada in reaction to the emotionally charged drama of Abstract Expressionism. It resulted in a more controlled art that made use of broad areas of flat colour. The influence of film and television could be seen in works by artists like Michael Snow, Joyce Wieland, and Gordon Rayner. In 1967 Michael Snow's experimental film *Wavelength,* helped define the genre of Structural film.

Painting had dominated Canadian art since the Group of Seven. By the 1960s new genres — process art, earth art, and performance art arose. Both sculpture and printmaking began to take on more significance, stimulated in part by commissions from large corporations and the government. In 1964, for instance, $105 000 was paid for Canadian paintings and sculptures to adorn the new Toronto International Airport. In 1968, General Idea was founded by A.A. Bronson, F. Partz, and J. Zontal. They worked collectively to examine mass media, pop culture, and the role of artists.

In the 1960s, Montreal was the centre of a flourishing, vibrant art community. The first museum in Canada devoted to contemporary art, the Musée d'Art Contemporain, was founded there in 1964. It was also in Montreal during Expo '67, the World's Fair celebrating Canada's Centennial, that the country's maturing art was made visible to the whole world.

▲ ALFRED PELLAN *Végétaux Marins*, 1964, oil on panel, 125 x 85 cm
Collection of the Corporation of the City of Kingston, Ontario. Photo: Larry Ostrom

It is important to take all the time necessary to do the picture well. I admit to being a slow painter, provided that a good picture comes from it.

A painter should be able to master his resources: if you are not in control of the techniques, the techniques will control you.

When I was teaching I sharpened the awareness of my students, I sowed uneasiness, I stimulated research: and the students learned to observe, to question themselves, to make their own discoveries. Lacking the complex of the prophet or the manitou, I did not want disciples behind me.

— Alfred Pellan, in *Contemporary Painting* by William Withrow, 1972

▲ Photo: Alfred Pellan

1962

The Region Gallery, London, Ontario is opened and run by Greg Curnoe – first artist-run gallery

1962

Norval Morrisseau exhibits at Pollock Gallery in Toronto – First Nations artist accepted as part of the mainstream Canadian professional art scene

1962

David Mirvish opens modernist gallery in Toronto

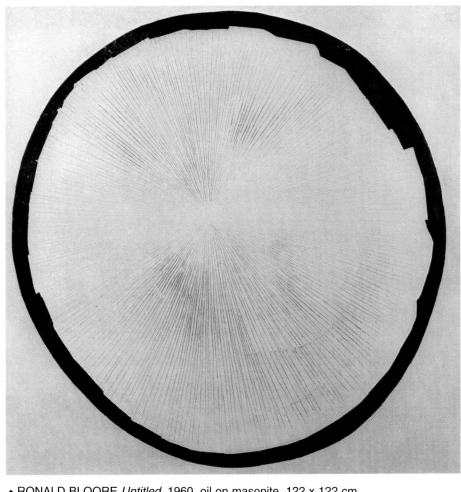

▲ RONALD BLOORE *Untitled,* 1960, oil on masonite, 122 x 122 cm
Reproduced with permission

▲ Photo: Ronald Bloore

I really, in a sense, don't think about it at all. It's not my problem to worry about it [work]…it just goes on and on. When people say to me, "You are down to twenty white lines on a page. What's the next phase?"…That is not their problem…that is my problem.

I do not worry about it…solutions come first. I begin to find I have a vocabulary of basic elements and use a kind of visual language…a visual alphabet. I don't care about the past.

— Ronald Bloore, *Contemporary Painting,* William Withrow, 1972

1960
–
1969

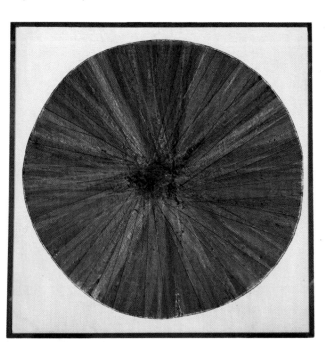

▲ ART MCKAY *Flux*, 1964, enamel and masonite, 121.5 cm x 121.5 cm
The Edmonton Art Gallery Collection. Purchased 1969

▶ CLAUDE TOUSIGNANT *Gong-88,* 1967, liquitex on canvas, 223.5 cm
Art Gallery of Ontario. Gift from the McLean Foundation 1968

1963

Ontario Arts Council established – largest provincial arts funding organization

1964

Musée d'art contemporain de Montréal is founded by the Ministry of Quebec Cultural Affairs

1965

Work by Guido Molinari is included in The Responsive Eye exhibition at the Museum of Modern Art, N.Y.

▸ JACK BUSH *Dazzle Red*, 1965, oil on canvas, 205.7 x 264.2 cm
Art Gallery of Ontario. Purchase, Corporations' Subscription Endowment, 1966

◂ MICHAEL SNOW *Expo Walking Woman*, 1967, polished stainless steel over plywood core; 11 component parts: stretch piece (silhouette) stainless steel: 228.6 x 71.3 x 243.8 cm; stretch piece (block) corner piece, fibre shell and stainless steel: 228.6 x 100.5 x 71.1 cm; 6 single figures, stainless steel: 228.6 x 71.8 x 2.5; 1 double figure, stainless steel: 228.6 x 71.3 x 2.5; 1 door piece (blank silhouette) stainless steel: 228.6 x 71.3 x 2.5
Art Gallery of Ontario. Gift of the Province of Ontario, 1968

"This business of framing derives from a series running from the first 'Walking Woman' paintings (where the woman was framed, cut-off) to the last highly polished 'Walking Woman' sculptures at Expo (which framed within themselves the reflected outside action)."

— Michael Snow, in an interview with Dorothy Cameron taped on 23 May 1967 and first published in "*Walking Woman Works*: Michael Snow 1961-67," in *Sculpture '67*, Agnes Etherington Art Centre, Kingston 1983

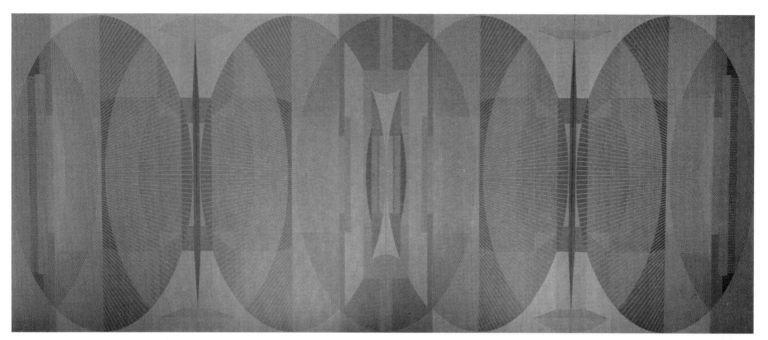

▲ BRIAN FISHER *Night Flight* (mural), 1968, polymer acrylic on fibreglass panels, 120 x 288 in
Department of Transport, Montreal

▼ HAROLD TOWN *Great Divide*, 1965, oil & lucite on canvas, 228.6 x 134.0 cm
Art Gallery of Ontario. Purchase, Corporations' Subscription Endowment, 1966

Art has never produced a more confident or more ambitious generation than the one now emerging. New materials and new forms of art, such as those now exhibited at the City Hall sculpture show, suggest what is happening.

But these are only the immediately visible signs of a whole new attitude to art.

The young artists have set out to question not only past and present styles in art but also, and more important, the very idea of what art is about.

They are possessed by the idea that today, in art, anything is possible.

At the same time, they have come to regard the whole idea of "Canadian art" as anachronistic. They see no relation between what they produce and what the artists of the Canadian past have created.

They regard themselves as part of the world art scene, and expect that eventually the world — which, in art means New York — will accept them on their own terms....

The new attitude stems partly from the nature of today's art scene. The market is richer than ever before, the attention given a young artist is greater than at any time in the past. But the demands on the artist are more urgent.

The art market is geared to revolution. To be called serious and important, the artist of 1967 must conceive and create his own world; fresh ideas mean everything.

...They [artists] see themselves not as Canadians but as part of the international scene, and in their own minds their work is set beside the best in the world...

The new artists are a generation without ties. They feel themselves unbound to country, region, art style, or art history. Their ambitions have no limits.

— Robert Fulford, "The New Artists: Audacious Rebels in a Rich Market" *The Toronto Daily Star*, 1 July 1967

1960 — 1969

1966

Carmen Lamanna Gallery
opens in Toronto

1966

Jack Chambers, Greg Curnoe, John Boyle, Kim Ondaatje and
others form CARFAC – Canadian Artists Representation/Front
des artists canadiens in London, Ontario

1966

*The Medium is the Message: An
Inventory of Effects* by Marshall
McLuhan and Quentin Fiore published

▲ CLAUDE BREEZE *Transmission Difficulties: The Operation,*
1968, acrylic on canvas, 172.4 x 239.0 cm
National Gallery of Canada, Ottawa. Purchased 1969

"Canada's not ready for painters like me just yet. I'm too tough,
I guess. It doesn't bother me that no one is buying my paintings. I'm not painting for people who live in apartment blocks.
Only 10 per cent of people who buy paintings in Canada really
care. The rest are just buying prestige…

We've got to learn to change paintings, like the
Europeans do. Right now, Canadians — people in Vancouver
anyway — are a little Mickey Mouse. You know what I mean?

But that'll change. The hippies will change it.

It's getting a little better for painters right now. The
Canada Council is doing a good job. They have people in different cities, watching the local scene, talking to painters,
buying something once in a while. That's good: and there are
the murals for public buildings. That's good too."

— Claude Breeze, in an interview with Val Sears, 1967

▲ JOYCE WIELAND *Reason over Passion,* 1968,
quilted cotton, 256.5 x 302.3 cm
The National Gallery of Canada, Ottawa. Purchased 1970

◀ PITSEOLAK ASHOONA *Inukshuk Builders*, 1967, stonecut, proof II (edition: 50) on laid, kozo paper, 61.9 x 70 cm
Canadian Museum of Civilization (S93-11 618)

▼ CHRISTOPHER PRATT *Shop on an Island*, 1969, oil on board, 81.3 x 91.4 cm
Museum London (79A.16). Gift of Mr. & Mrs. John H. Moore of London through the Ontario Heritage Foundation 1979

1960 – 1969

35

The 1970s was the decade of the baby boomers. The majority of Canadians were under 30 and they had money to spend. Canada had developed a reputation as a safe, peaceful country, and draft resisters from America flooded university campuses to avoid the Vietnam War. American influence was everywhere causing the government to institute Canadian content quotas to protect Canadian culture. Marshall McLuhan became a cultural icon and people around the world quoted his, "the medium is the message" theories of communications. The flood of ideas ushered in by mass communications and rapid technological change brought with it social upheaval, terrorism, and separatism. The Toronto Eaton Centre was built as a monument to consumerism. Michael Snow's sculpture of a flock of Canadian geese was installed in its atrium and became a Canadian icon.

In 1972 the National Museums Corporation was established to oversee the business of cultural activities. Government funding ensured that Canadian artists were able to explore avant-garde artforms like conceptual art, installation art, video and performance art. Alternative art galleries like A Space in Toronto run by artists, and Véhicule in Montreal provided an audience and market for contemporary art. The changing gallery structure was accompanied by "independent" curators who put together shows outside of the larger public institutions.

During the 1970s, artists across Canada continued to explore abstraction and minimalism. There were also artists like Alex Colville, Mary Pratt, and Jack Chambers who pushed the boundaries of representation in their meticulous, high-realist paintings. Conceptual art, begun in the 60s by people like Iain Baxter and the N.E. Thing Company, reacted to the commercialization of the art world and pushed the boundaries of art. Artists began to exploit the possibilities of photography and sculpture gained greater acceptance becoming more innovative and creative. A boost for women's issues occurred in 1971 when Joyce Wieland became the first living female artist to have a retrospective at the National Gallery. A low point was the controversy over the heavy-handed censorship by Montreal mayor Jean Drapeau when he ordered the destruction of the CORRIDART: dans la rue Sherbrooke art exhibition in 1976.

▲ JACK SHADBOLT *Fetish*, 1970,
mixed media on paper, 149 x 104.1 cm
Firestone Art Collection (FAC 1169): The Ottawa Art Gallery. Donated by the Ontario Heritage Foundation to the City of Ottawa. Photo: Time Wickens

▼ Museum of Anthropology, Vancouver, B.C., 1973-76
Photo: Bill McLennan

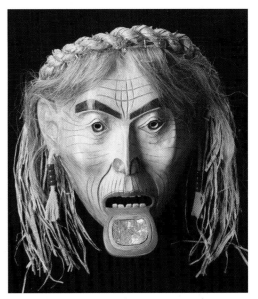

◄ MARY PRATT *Salmon on Saran*, 1974, oil on panel, 45.7 x 50.8 cm
Photo: Courtesy Mary Pratt

At first I felt badly about having to resort to slides. All the spontaneous delight with my subject seemed to be gone, and the calculating way I was able to discard, plan and design was foreign to me. However, this new method of working allowed me to paint things I couldn't have attempted before, because of light and time. And so I decided to let other people worry about the validity of using slides. I didn't know in those days that other people used them.

— Mary Pratt, in *Some Canadian Women Artists* by Mayo Graham, National Gallery of Canada, 1975

▲ FREDA DIESING *Haida Elderly Noble Woman Mask*, 1974, birch and red cedar bark, paint, abalone, 11 x 23.5 x 21.3 cm
Royal British Columbia Museum. RBCM Catalogue #15057

◄ MICHAEL SNOW *Flight Stop*, 1979, Toronto Eaton Centre
Photo: Courtesy Brett Miller

▲ JOE FAFARD *A Merchant of Pense*, 1973, ceramic, 41 x 25 x 38 cm
Glenbow Museum, Calgary

1974

General Idea founds Art Metropole in Toronto – a non-profit contemporary visual arts centre

1974

The History of Painting in Canada: Toward a People's Art by Barry Lord presents the first socialist view of Canadian art history

1974

The Society for the Study of Architecture in Canada/la société pour l'étude de l'architecture au Canada founded

▲ MELVIN CHARNEY
View of the Installation *Les Maisons de la rue Sherbrooke*, Corridart Exhibition Montreal, negative exposed, 1976, chromogenic colour print, sheet 40.7 x 50.8 cm, image 36.4 x 49.8 cm
Canadian Centre for Architecture, Montreal. Gift of Melvin Charney

The Leonard & Bina Ellen Art Gallery of Concordia University is pleased to present the exhibition CORRIDART: Revisited from July 12 to August 18, 2001.

This exhibition marks the twenty-fifth anniversary of the demolition of COR-RIDART: dans la rue Sherbrooke. This "corridor of art" along Sherbrooke Street was the major project of the Arts and Culture programme for Montreal's 1976 Summer Olympics. The organizer and guiding spirit of the event was the artist Melvin Charney. The presentation was scheduled to be on display from July 7 to 31, along a five-mile route from Atwater Avenue to the Olympic site. Its visual art projects and performance areas created an outdoor linear museum which simultaneously recalled the cultural history of Sherbrooke Street. The presentation was united by the narrative of the scaffolding and panels of Memoire de la rue. After only one week, however, the exhibition was ordered destroyed by Montreal mayor Jean Drapeau and his Executive Council in a political act of censorship that has come to overshadow the artwork as well as the ambitions of the exhibition itself.

— Bulletin from Leonard & Bina Ellen Art Gallery

▶ MIYUKI TANOBE
The Québec Carnival, 1976, nihonga
Photo: Courtesy Miyuki Tanobe

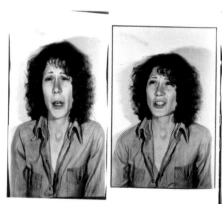

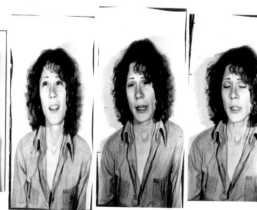

◀ SUZY LAKE
Maquette for Mephisto Waltz: from the photo installation *Are You Talking to Me?*, 1979, black and white photographs with acrylic, 279 x 109 cm and smaller
Art Gallery of Hamilton. Gift of Mr. & Mrs. Edwin L. Stringer, 1982

1976
Michael Snow first Canadian to have major exhibition of avant-garde artist's film at N.Y. Museum of Modern Art

1976
The Print and Drawing Council of Canada formed

1977
Canadian Art Therapy Association formed in Toronto

1979
Art Gallery of Toronto hosts Judy Chicago's The Dinner Party exhibition

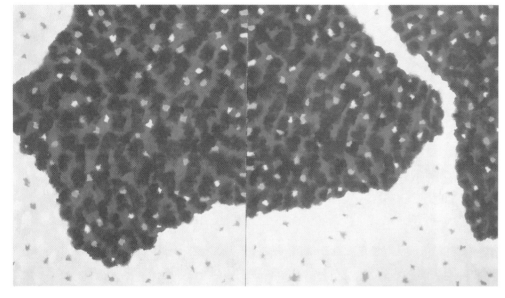

◀ GERSHON ISKOWITZ *Autumn B,* 1978, oil on canvas, 168.7 x 307.3 cm
Robert McLaughlin Gallery, Oshawa

"My recent work using negative images, makes this vital aspect (i.e. the casting process) more direct. One is aware of the enclosing space that a person occupied and becomes conscious of the person and how the space was defined."

— Colette Whiten, *artscanada,* May/June, 1977

▼ COLETTE WHITEN *Family,* 1977-78, plaster and burlap, life size
Photo: G. Dick, Courtesy Colette Whiten

"People say, oh, Gershon Iskowitz is an abstract artist. I hear that a lot of times. But it's a whole realistic world. It lives, moves… it has to move or it's dead! I see those things…the experience, out in the field, of looking up in the trees or in the sky, of looking down from the height of a helicopter. So what you do is try to make a composition of all those things, make some kind of reality: like the trees should belong to the sky, and the ground should belong to the trees, and the ground should belong to the sky. Everything has to be united. That's painting…my work comes visually from memories, and the colour also is self-invented…it's something you invent on your own. Okay, it's a lot to do with landscape, but you've got to project yourself into that form. I paint the country in my own way."

— Gershon Iskowitz, interview with Merike Weiler, Iskowitz exhibition catalogue, Glenbow-Alberta Institute, 1957

▼ ALEX COLVILLE *Swimming Dog and Canoe,* 1979, acrylic polymer emulsion, 53.4 x 119.4 cm
Photo: Courtesy A.C. Fine Art

Possibly the most significant political change for Canadians in the 20th century was the patriation of the Constitution and the inclusion of the Charter of Rights and Freedoms in 1982. The process left a deep rift between Quebec and the rest of Canada that fueled the fires of separatism. The Charter became a defining icon of Canadian nationalism. Immigration continued to change the face of Canada, stimulated by the government's official policy of multiculturalism. New Canadians of the 1980s included eastern Europeans, Chinese, Vietnamese, Latin Americans, South Asians, and Somalis. They brought with them new foods, religions, and social attitudes. The "me" decade, as the 1980s was called, saw a rising emphasis on individual rights and personal freedoms. Adolescents, dubbed Generation X, were the first generation to grow up with computers, video games, and the Internet, making them the most experienced media generation in history.

A wealth of artworks, films, and videos was produced in the 1980s. Issues of identity, environment, memory and originality continued to be explored and expanded upon, but with a new focus on ambiguity and abstraction.

In 1983, Le Centre International d'art contemporain de Montreal, was established to promote contemporary art. In 1985 it organized a groundbreaking show, 100 Days of Contemporary Art, that brought fresh energy to the Canadian art scene.

Neo-Expressionism was introduced to Canada by Vancouver artists Attila Richard Lukacs, Angela Grossmann, and Vicky Marshall and specifically in Toronto by the ChromaZone/Chromatique Collective (1981-85) whose members included Andy Fabo, Sybil Goldstein, and Rae Johnson. Neo-Expressionism revived interest in the figure.

This was the decade when female artists including Betty Goodwin, Jana Sterbak, and Gathie Falk won greater recognition for their work, and artists like Carl Beam, Robert Houle, and Joane Cardinal-Shubert struggled to be taken seriously as contemporary artists who "happen to be Indian." By the end of the decade barriers that had excluded some from the mainstream art world began to come down.

▲ DAVID BLACKWOOD *Fire Down on the Labrador,* 1980, etching and aqua-tint on wove paper, 93 x 62.9 cm
Art Gallery of Ontario. Gift of David and Anita Blackwood, Port Hope, ON 1999

"Prints are a democratic art form because of the multiple (reproductions). I print in editions of 50, or more recently 75, which brings down the cost. Painting is very elitist — only a wealthy person can buy it, and then it disappears from view."

— David Blackwood, *Toronto Star*, 6 April 2002

1983

Le Centre International d'Art Contemporain de
Montréal (CIAC) is founded – main objective is to
encourage and assist research in contemporary art

1983

The Warehouse Show is launched
in Vancouver as an alternative to
the art establishment

1985

The Canadian Centre for
Architecture founded in
Montreal

◂ AIKO SUZUKI *Lyra,* 1981, permanent fibre
installation at the Metro Reference Library
Photo: Courtesy Aiko Suzuki

"I feel like a dancer when I make these pieces. The trouble with paintings is that they limit you in the ways you can move through space. For me, these suspensions don't even assume their final shapes until I'm up on a ladder poking at them and twisting them into the spatial form I want for them."

— Aiko Suzuki, *Globe and Mail,* 1 May 1985

▸ BILL REID *Phyllidula: The Shape of Frogs to Come,*
1984-85, red cedar, paint, 43.1 x 124.5 cm
Vancouver Art Gallery, VAG 86.16. Photo: Trevor Mills

▾ ATTILA RICHARD LUKACS
I'l y'avait quinze ans que je n'ai pas fait ça, 1985,
enamel, oil, tar on canvas, 254 x 487.5 cm
Vancouver Art Gallery, VAG 85.91.1-4. Photo: Trevor Mills

1980
–
1989

41

1985

CIAC presents 100 Days of Contemporary Art in Montreal – brings national and international artists together in one show

1985

Young Romantics show at Vancouver Art Gallery features Neo-Expressionism

1986

Lawren Harris' work included in The Spiritual in Art: Abstract Painting show at L.A. County Museum of Art

◀ GATHIE FALK *Pieces of Water: Libya,* 1980-81, oil on canvas, 198.1 x 167.6 cm
Vancouver Art Gallery, VAG 86.202. Photo: Trevor Mills and Teresa Healy

"When I painted this picture I was attempting to touch base with things like grandmothers' gardens and prairie folk painting — note the 'peacock painting' on the door of the house and the 'tree of virtue' in the front yard. But the dream home is in the mind, not in a castle — even a small home can be beautiful."

— David Thauberger, *Home Truths, A Celebration of of Family Life by Canada's Best-Loved Painters* by Joan Murray

▶ DAVID THAUBERGER *Dream Home (Ethnic Version),* 1980, acrylic on canvas, 115 x 172.7 cm
MacKenzie Art Gallery, University of Regina Collection Gift of Douglas Rawlinson. Photo: Don Hall

42

1988

Fire Down on the Labrador by David Blackwood auctioned for $22 000 – most valuable Canadian print ever sold

1988

The new building for the National Gallery of Canada opens in Ottawa, Ontario

1988

The Canadian Museum of Civilization building opens in Hull, Quebec

▲ JOANE CARDINAL-SCHUBERT
Four Directions: War Shirts, My Mother's Vision, 1986, oil, oil pastel, chalk, graphite on paper, 80.7 x 121 cm each sheet
Canadian Museum of Civilization

▼ MANASIE AKPALIAPIK *Respecting the Circle*, 1989, whalebone, ivory, dark grey stone, antler, baleen, rust stone, horn, 52.0 x 71.4 x 40.0 cm
Art Gallery of Ontario, Gift of Samual and Esther Sarick

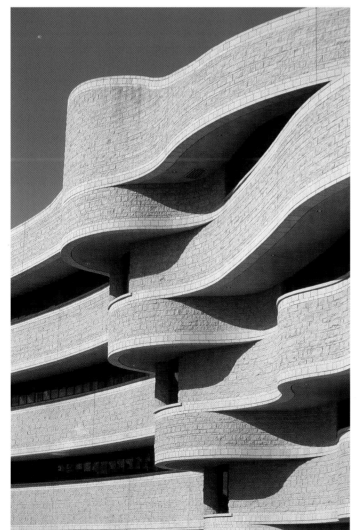

◄ MUSEUM OF CIVILIZATION
Hull, Quebec, 1983, designed by Douglas Cardinal
Photo: Museum of Civilization

1980
—
1989

43

1990

The National Gallery of Canada pays
1.76 million dollars for *Voice of Fire*
painted by Barnett Newman in 1967

As the 90s began Canada slipped into a recession. A general sense of unrest gripped the country. Groups that had been marginalized in preceding decades made gains in many areas, but not without a fight. During the 1990s aboriginal issues remained at the forefront. In 1993 Nunavut was created accompanied by the largest land claims settlement in Canada — $1.1 billion to be paid out between 1993 and 2007, and title to 1.9 million square kilometres of land and water. The use of information technology grew steadily with 4.2 million households owning computers by 1997. The Internet and high speed access changed the way people worked, shopped, and did business. Music, books, and art could be downloaded to the computer. This raised issues about copyright and intellectual property. By the end of the decade the threat of separatism had subsided, the economy was bouncing back and Canadians were generally flourishing.

Issues of the body, identity, technology, memory, and the environment informed the work of Post-Modern artists during the 1990s. Photography continued to be exploited by artists like Jeff Wall and Ian Wallace. They produced photoconceptual art that used photography as the foundation of the work, but not the end product. In Vancouver, Artropolis advanced the accomplishments of the 1983 Warehouse Show. In 1992 their exhibition, held in a former department store, had possibly the largest attendance of any art show in Vancouver's history. Across Canada artists worked in painting, photography, sculpture, film, video, installation, and printmaking. By the end of the decade there was a strong First Nations presence as they experienced a renaissance. In the Arctic artists represented more than 20% of the Inuit population. For them art was an exportable commodity necessary for survival. They continued to seek innovation while dealing with issues of tradition and commercialization.

At the end of the 20th century Canadian art had found a respected place on the world stage. Women and men of all races and beliefs had become valued contributors. Early in the century the Group of Seven had fought to establish a distinctly Canadian art. By 1999 Canadian art had long since abandoned Canadianism and become world art.

▲ BILL REID *The Spirit of the Haida Gwaii,* 1991,
second cast, 1994, patinated bronze, 3.9 x 6.1 x 3.5 m
Vancouver International Airport Authority

Here we are at last, a long way from the Haida Gwaii, not too sure where we are or where we're going, still squabbling and vying for position in the boat, but somehow managing to appear to be heading in some direction; at least the paddles are together, and the man in the middle seems to have some vision of what is to come.

As for the rest, they are superficially more or less what they always were, symbols of another time when the Haidas, all ten thousands of them, knew they were the greatest of all nations.

— Bill Reid, Foreword to *The Spirit of the Gwaii, Bill Reid's Masterpiece*

▲ GENERAL IDEA *One Year of AZT,* 1991, background: 1825 units of vacuum-formed styrene with vinyl, each unit 12.7 cm x 31.7 cm x 6.3 cm; foreground: five units of enameled fiberglass
National Gallery of Canada, Ottawa. Purchased 1995

1991	1993	1994
Vanitas: Flesh Dress for an Albino Anorectic by Jana Sterbak shown at the National Gallery of Canada	Parliament passes the Nunavut Act	*A History of Canadian Architecture* by Harold Kalman published

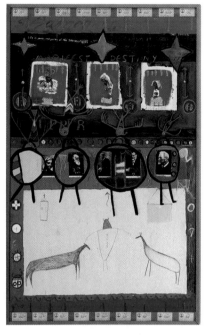

▲ JANE ASH POITRAS *A Sacred Prayer for a Sacred Island*, 1991, oil paint, collages of photographs, photocopies and printed papers, blackboard acrylic, wax crayon, eagle feather and five dollar-bill on canvas, side panels each 187.9 cm x 127 cm, centre panel 187.3 cm x 437.5 cm
National Gallery of Canada, Ottawa. Purchased 1995

"People ask you who you are and you don't know what to say. You look out on the world, and it's all white and it's not you. And you are always living with this anxiety that if you don't do what they say, you'll be thrown out on the street."

— Jane Ash Poitras, *Canadian Art,* Fall 1994

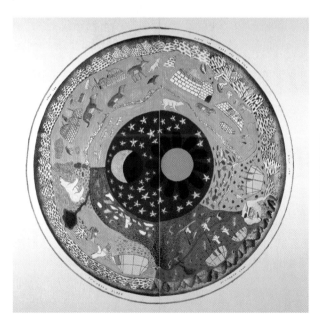

▲ KENOJUAK ASHEVAK *Nunavut (Our Land)*, 1992, hand-coloured lithograph, proof (edition: 3) on wove paper watermark, 120 x 134 cm
Gift of the Department of Indian Affairs and Northern Development, 1994, Cape Dorset 1993, No.1. Canadian Museum of Civilization (S99-5423)

"I have always enjoyed making carvings, but now I just sit around because my hands aren't good any more for that kind of task...It's as if my hands have gotten back at me..."

— Kenojuak Ashevak, *Inuit Women Artists: Voices from Cape Dorset*

▼ GERALD FERGUSON *Fish and Door,* 1992, enamel on canvas and painted wood, 213.3 cm x 223.5 cm
Art Gallery of Nova Scotia. Purchased with funds provided by Trimark Investment Management, Inc., Toronto, 1994

1990
—
1999

45

1995

The first Canadian Internet art gallery started by
Andrew Wysotski in Oshawa, Ontario

1995

Art Metropole transfers its collection of 13 000
items to the National Gallery of Canada

▲ SALLY MICHENER *Alice, Donna, Helen, John and Adam*, 1993-94,
ceramic covered with pottery shards, tiles, glass and mirror,
H 6'1" x W 10' x D 5' (group), each figure is human height
UBC Museum of Anthropology. Photo: Bill McLennan

Photo: Courtesy Sally Michener

"Tiles glazed and shaped by me. Thrown
away bits of tiles and pottery from friends and
students, crockery and chinaware bits from
many kitchens, mirror or other glass bits
found in my wide search, and historic shards
discovered on the tidal banks of the Fraser
River. I really enjoy the blending of these
materials. I think about their previous uses
and by whom, and it all becomes a statement
of what we are all made of — our past, our
present — mixed in a mozaic."

— Sally Michener, *Great Work! An Overview of
Contemporary British Columbia Artists*, Compiled
by Melanie Gold, Portraiture by Rob Kruyt

▶ MACAULAY ETELI *Stage One*, 1994,
acrylic gel on canvas, 20 x 30 in
Photo: Courtesy Eteli Artworks

"Art is something that is within me. It was
fun. Creative fun. Something to keep me out
of mischief. I show aspects of the cultural life
of African peoples. In Africa, everything we
do, we put into art."

— Macaulay Eteli

46

◄ AGANETHA DYCK *Lady in Waiting: The Extended Wedding Party*, 1995, glass and honeycomb
Photo: Courtesy Aganetha Dyck

There's a tremendous power in a hive. It's like a pulsing intelligence. I just allowed chaos and chance to happen....And while I feel warmly towards bees, it's a cruel world in a hive. They don't have senior citizens' homes in hives.

— Chris Dafoe, "Minding Her Beeswax," *Globe and Mail,* 28 February 1996

▶ TED HARRISON *Quiet Village*, 1995, acrylic, 92 x 61.5 cm
Hollander York Gallery. Photo: Courtesy Wingate Arts Ltd.

It must be understood that I have been trained as an academic painter in the old tradition, drawing from the casts of ancient Greek sculptures... repeating intricate exercises in linear perspective, mathematically precise and accurate to a fraction of an inch.

— Ted Harrison, *The World of Ted Harrison,* catalogue of an exhibition held at The Art Gallery of Greater Victoria, 20 September to 17 November 1996

...the Canadian art market as we know it today could simply dry up...We will probably start hearing about "schools" of artists we never knew existed, and styles and associations that have never been publicized — all in the interests of keeping the market active? Modern paintings will almost certainly appear more often at auction, and something we have been advocating for years, today's "minor" painters with good pedigree, will now start rising to the ranks of more recognized and desirable artists.

— "Why Not the Group of Twenty Seven or The Painters Eleven Hundred?" *Art Market Report,* December/January 1998

▶ NOEL HARDING *The Elevated Wetlands,* 1997-98,
6 sculptures made of expanded polystyrene foam, acrylic stucco coating, solar-powered irrigation system, recycled plastic soil structure, native plants, and water from the Don River
Photo location: Taylor Creek Park, Toronto

1990
—
1999

47

Into the 21st Century

◀ Logo for CYBERMUSE (the online gallery of the National Gallery of Canada)
http://cybermuse.gallery.ca

THE SANDERS SHAKESPEARE: Adventures at the Canadian Conservation Institute

www.canadianart.ca

CANADIAN

a|r|t

Spring 2002 · Volume 19 · Number 1 · $6.95

The devil
IN Ms. GRIFFITHS
by R. M. Vaughan

Nasgaard on Richter
Kingston's Museopathy
Douglas Cardinal

Eli Langer Nicolas Baier Roberta McNaughton Daniel Olson Lynne Cohen

◀ Cover: *Canadian Art*, Spring 2002, Vol.19 No.1
Reprinted with permission

▾ NATALKA HUSAR *Horseshoes and Waves*, 2001, oil on linen with zippers, 218 x 142 cm
Photo: Christopher Chown; Courtesy Natalka Husar

A rare painting by Paul Kane sets a new records for Canadian art

A rare Paul Kane portrait brought from England has sold for nearly $5.1 million — more than twice the previous record price for a Canadian painting.

As the gavel fell last night, the crowd erupted in a round of applause.

Fierce bidding for Kane's *Scene In The Northwest — Portrait,* executed in the winter of 1845-46, reached $4.6 million in a three-way duel among two American buyers on the telephone and Winnipeg art dealer David Loch, who bid with a subtle nod of the head from the back of the room. A fourth buyer dropped out of the bidding at $900,000.

When the dust settled, Loch — who's known to represent media mogul Ken Thomson at art auctions — got the prize. Adding in the buyer's premium…Kane's portrait will actually cost $5,062,500 — 10 times its pre-sale estimate.

The highest amount previously paid for a Canadian painting was $2.2 million for Lawren Harris' *Baffin Island,* purchased last year by Thomson. He exhibits his extensive collection at his gallery in the Bay's Queen Street store.

— Judy Stoffman, *Toronto Star*, 26 February 2002, reprinted with permission

$5,062,500

A rare painting by Paul Kane
sets a new record for Canadian art

48

◂ KELLY MARK *War Pigs*, 2002,
video – 7 min 55 sec.
Photo: Courtesy Kelly Mark

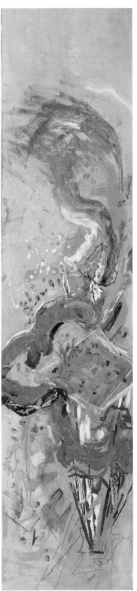

Amid the loss of lives, the disaster felling the Twin Towers of the World Trade Center in New York six-months ago destroyed numerous artworks and killed Michael Richards, a 38-year-old sculptor, as he was sleeping in his studio.

Richards was one of 15 artists who had been allocated empty office space in Tower 1 by the Lower Manhattan Cultural Center. Susanna Heller, a 40-something Montreal-born painter, was another.

On Sept. 11th, Heller was about to head to Manhattan over the bridge from her Green Point, Brooklyn home, a trek that usually would have brought her to the World Trade Center around 10 A.M. She was, however, late, and became a witness, not a victim, of the tragedy.

She remembers the remarkable clarity of the sky that day.

"It was really a glazed, glowy, shiny kind of thing," she says. "The whole fall in New York was like that, but especially those few weeks before. It was a painful, tragically beautiful time.

"I could watch it all come down from where I was in Brooklyn. It's so easy to talk about it now, but watching (the towers collapse) is seeing your grandmother shot in front of your eyes. But what can you do about it after?"

Heller, based in the New York area since 1978, was allocated studio space in the World Trade Center four years ago.

"It was supposed to be for four months but it ended up being for a lot longer."

Before the terrorist attacks, she was in the process of moving back to her home studio and had already removed most of her works from the tower, although she lost three in the collapse.

Not lost are her memories.

In one sense, *Fractured Ascension* and *Haunting*, two of her works now at the Olga Korper Gallery (17 Morrow Ave.) until April 3, represent a pre- and post- Sept. 11 view of New York, although both were finished after the tragedy. In another sense, they are both part of the New York story Heller has been painting for years.

— Peter Goddard, "Art By Numbers" *Toronto Star*, 16 March 2002

◂ SUSANNA HELLER
Fractured Ascension, 2002, oil on canvas
Photo: Courtesy Olga Korper Gallery

▸ SUSANNA HELLER
Haunting, 2002, oil on canvas
Photo: Courtesy Olga Korper Gallery

Artists Featured in this Book

Ashevak, Kenojuak (b.1927) is an Inuit printmaker and sculptor who works in Cape Dorset. Famous for her images of owls and Inuit life, she is possibly the most internationally known Inuit artist.

Ashoona, Pitseolak (1904-1983) was an Inuit printmaker, textile artist, and sculptor who worked in Cape Dorset.

Bayefsky, Aba (1923-2001) was a painter and teacher who worked in Toronto. He was only 19 when he became one of the Official War Artists of World War II.

Beatty, J.W. (1869-1941) was a Toronto painter, printmaker, and art teacher who was one of the Official War Artists.

Binning, B.C. (1909-1976) was a Vancouver painter, teacher, and curator. He is known for his drawings and decorative abstractions.

Bloore, Ronald (b. 1925) is a painter, sculptor, and muralist who has worked in Toronto and Regina. He was a member of the Regina Five — a group of five artists from Regina featured in a 1961 exhibition at the National Gallery of Canada.

Blackwood, David (b. 1941) is an internationally respected printmaker known for his etchings that focus on old Newfoundland stories told by fishermen when he was growing up. He lives in Port Hope, Ontario.

Bobak, Molly Lamb (b. 1922) is a painter, printmaker, teacher, and writer who works in Fredericton, New Brunswick.

Borduas, Paul-Émile (1905-1960) was born in Saint-Hilaire, Quebec. He worked with Ozias Leduc who was his inspiration. He was widely denounced for writing the Refus Global.

Breeze, Claude (b. 1938) is a painter and printmaker who began on the west coast and moved to Toronto in 1976. He teaches at York University.

Brooker, Bertram (1888-1955) was a Toronto painter who was among the first Canadian artists to experiment with abstract painting.

Brittain, Miller (1912-1968) was a painter and muralist who worked in Saint John, New Brunswick. He is known for his images of life in Saint John.

Brymner, William (1855-1925) worked in both Ottawa and Montreal. He was a painter and muralist known for his careful draughtsmanship. He taught at the Art Association of Montreal from 1886-1921.

Bush, Jack (1909-1977) was a Toronto artist known for his colour-field paintings. He was a founding member of Painters Eleven.

Cahén, Oscar (1916-1956) was an Ontario artist who was one of the founding members of Painters Eleven. He died in a car accident three years after the group was formed.

Cardinal, Douglas (b. 1934) is a Métis architect famous for his distinctive, organic designs.

Cardinal-Schubert, Joane (b. 1942) is a Blood (Blackfoot) artist and First Nations activist. She is known for her paintings and installations of contemporary First Nations experiences.

Carlyle, Florence (1864-1923) was a Woodstock, Ontario artist. She studied in Paris and was known for her paintings of figures.

Carr, Emily (1871-1945) was a painter and writer from Victoria, British Columbia. She produced a large body of Native themed paintings; after meeting with the Group of Seven at the age of 57, her work became more "freely expressive of natural rhythms."

Clapp, William Henry (1879-1954) was an American-born artist who worked in Montreal and studied with William Brymner. He took many painting trips with Clarence Gagnon.

Clark, Paraskeva (1898-1986) grew up and studied art in Russia. She came to Toronto in 1931. Her strong sense of social-realism influenced other Canadian painters.

Colville, Alex (b. 1920) is a painter and printmaker who works in Nova Scotia. He is known for introducing Magic Realism to Canada.

Comfort, Charles (1900-1994) was a printmaker and painter who worked in Toronto. He was the director of the National Art Gallery from 1960-1965.

Coonan, Emily (1885-1971) was a Montreal painter who studied with William Brymner.

Cullen, Maurice (1866-1934) was a Montreal artist who studied in Paris. He is famous for his paintings of Montreal cities, snow-covered landscapes, and images of Newfoundland. His impressionist style influenced other Canadian painters and helped prepare the public for the new approach to painting ushered in by the Group of Seven.

Dallaire, Jean-Philippe (1916-1965) was a painter, illustrator, and muralist who worked in Quebec. He was influenced by Alfred Pellan and surrealism.

Dyck, Aganetha (b. 1937) is a Manitoba artist known for her wax and honeycomb covered sculptures. She collaborates with bees to show a "language of nature."

Erickson, Arthur (b. 1924) is an internationally respected architect known for his striking buildings and outspoken views about the future of Vancouver.

Eteli, Macaulay (b. 1956) is a Nigerian-born painter who settled in Canada in 1978.

Fafard, Joe (b. 1942) is a Saskatchewan artist best known for his realistic and satirical sculptures.

Falk, Gathie (b. 1928) is one of British Columbia's best known artists. She is internationally respected for her imaginative images of everyday things.

Ferguson, Gerald (b. 1937) is an American-born artist who has been working and teaching in Nova Scotia since 1968. He is best known for his abstract, conceptual paintings and installations.

Fisher, Brian (b. 1939) is a Vancouver born painter, muralist, and printmaker who studied with Ronald Bloore and Art McKay. He worked in western Canada until 1981 when he moved to Australia.

Fripp, Thomas (1864-1931) was a British Columbian painter known for his Rocky Mountain and Pacific coast scenes.

Fortin, Marc-Aurèl (1888-1970) was a painter and printmaker who worked in Montreal and Ste. Rose. He is known for his rural and urban Quebec scenes.

Gagnon, Clarence (1881-1924) was a Montreal painter, printmaker, and illustrator. He is famous for his 1933 illustrations for the book *Maria Chapdelaine* by Louis Hemon.

Roberts, Goodridge (1904-1974) was a painter and teacher who worked in Ottawa, Kingston, and Montreal. He was a founding member of the Contemporary Arts Society.

Harding, Noel (b. 1945) is an internationally respected artist who is known for his ability to present nature in unique ways. He is the youngest artist ever to have a major retrospective at the Art Gallery of Ontario.

Harris, Lawren P. (1910-1994) was the son of the Group of Seven's Lawren Harris. He is known for his landscapes, portraits, and murals.

Harrison, Ted (b. 1926) is an internationally respected artist and author famous for his colourful paintings of the Yukon. He received the Order of Canada for his contributions to Canadian culture.

Hébert, Louis-Philippe (1850-1917) was a Montreal sculptor. His monuments are at the Parliament building in Quebec City and in many Canadian cities.

Heward, Prudence (1896-1947) was a painter who worked in Montreal, Quebec, and Brockville, Ontario. She was a founding member of the Canadian Group of Painters.

Housser, Yvonne McKague (b. 1898) was a Toronto painter and teacher. She was a founding member of the Canadian Group of Painters.

Husar, Natalka (b. 1951) is a first generation Ukranian-Canadian who was born in New Jersey and moved to Toronto in 1973. She is known for her intense paintings that explore the immigrant experience.

Iskowitz, Gershon (1921-1988) was born in Poland and survived Auschwitz. He immigrated to Canada in 1949. He is best known for his large, light-filled canvases.

Jefferys, C.W. (1869-1951) was a York Mills, Ontario painter and illustrator. His historical drawings are found in many Canadian history books.

Lake, Suzy (b. 1947) is an internationally recognized artist who works in photography, performance, and video. She was a founding member of Vehicule Art in Montreal in 1971. She teaches at the University of Guelph.

Leduc, Fernand (b. 1916) is a Montreal painter who was a member of the Automatistes. He signed the Refus Global.

Leduc, Ozias (1864-1955) was a painter and muralist in Saint-Hilaire and Saint-Hyacinthe, Quebec. He had a great influence on Paul-Émile Borduas.

Lemieux, Jean-Paul (b. 1904) is a Quebec artist known for his landscape paintings of Charlevoix County and his portraits of important public figures.

Loring, Frances (1887-1968) was a sculptor who worked in Toronto. She studied in Europe and the U.S.

Lukacs, Attila Richard (b. 1962) is an Alberta-born artist who moved to New York in 1986. He is best known for his large paintings of skinheads and American military cadets.

Macdonald, Jock (1897-1960) was a painter who worked in Vancouver and Toronto where he taught at the Ontario College of Art. He was a founding member of the Canadian Group of Painters.

Mark, Kelly (b. 1967) is a Welland, Ontario artist who studied with Gerald Ferguson at the Nova Scotia College of Art and Design. She uses performance, installation, sculpture, and video to explore ordinary events.

McKay, Art (b. 1926) is a Regina painter known for his non-objective, complex work. He was a member of the Regina Five.

McLaughlin, Isabel (b.1903) was a painter who worked in Toronto and Oshawa. She was a founding member of the Canadian Group of Painters.

McNicoll, Helen (1879-1915) was a Montreal painter who studied with William Brymner and in England.

Michener, Sally (b. 1935) is a Vancouver artist and teacher who works primarily with clay, hand building her sculptures.

Morrice, James Wilson (1865-1924) was a Quebec painter who lived abroad for most of his life. He painted many scenes of Quebec, which he visited regularly.

Morris, Edmund (1871-1913) was a Toronto artist known for his paintings of historical subjects and portraits.

Mousseau, Jean-Paul (b. 1927) is a Montreal painter who studied with Paul-Émile Borduas. He was a member of the Automatistes.

Pellan, Alfred (1906-1988) was a Montreal painter and teacher. He encouraged artists to experiment and is credited with bringing modernism to Quebec.

Phillips, Walter J. (1884-1963) was a painter, illustrator, and printmaker who worked in Winnipeg and Calgary. He is known for his colour woodcut prints.

Poitras, Jane Ash (b. 1953) is a Chippewayan (Cree) artist known for her postmodern, mixed media explorations of the impact of colonialism and the spiritual strength of aboriginal peoples.

Pratt, Christopher (b. 1935) is a Newfoundland artist known for his stark, realist paintings, and prints.

Pratt, Mary (b. 1935) is a Newfoundland painter who creates meticulous images of domestic scenes and food.

Reid, Bill (1920-1998) was a Haida artist famous for his contributions to the late 20th century rebirth of Haida culture.

Roberts, Goodridge (1904-1974) was a painter and teacher who worked in Ottawa, Kingston, and Montreal. He was a founding member of the Contemporary Arts Society.

Savage, Anne (1896-1971) was a Montreal painter and teacher. She was a founding member of the Canadian Group of Painters.

Shadbolt, Jack (1909-1998) was a Vancouver painter, teacher, and activist known for his strong abstract paintings.

Snow, Michael (b.1929) is a Toronto artist internationally famous for his work with experimental film.

Suzor-Coté, Marc-Aurèle (1869-1937) was a Quebec painter, sculptor, and church decorator.

Suzuki, Aiko (b. 1937) is a Toronto artist known for her work with the Ontario Arts Council, the Academy of Canadian Cinema, and YTV.

Tanobe, Miyuki (b. 1937) is a Montreal artist known for her joyful images of Quebec society. She uses the ancient technique of nihonga which she learned in Japan.

Thauberger, David (b. 1948) is a Saskatchewan painter who creates serious/humorous images of prairie buildings.

Tousignant, Claude (b. 1932) is a Montreal artist famous for his hard-edge, abstract paintings.

Town, Harold (1924-1990) was a Toronto painter, printmaker, sculptor, and muralist. He wrote about art and artists, and was a member of Painters Eleven.

Vaillancourt, Armand (b. 1932) is a Quebec sculptor known for his formalist, abstract sculptures, and political activism.

Watkins, Margaret (1884-1969) was born in Hamilton and studied in New York. She was one of the first women to be hired to work in advertising in the 1920s.

Walker, Horatio (1858-1938) was an artist from Ile d'Orléans famous for his paintings of rural Quebec farm scenes.

Whiten, Colette (b. 1945) is one of Canada's leading sculptors. She teaches at the Ontario College of Art and Design.

Wood, Elizabeth Wyn (1903-1966) was an Ontario sculptor and a founding member of the Sculptors' Society of Canada. She became known as the Lawren Harris of Sculpture.

Wieland, Joyce (1931-1998) was a Toronto artist known for her strong sense of nationalism and work that combined "high art" and crafts.

Cover Story / William Ronald on his painting:

Pierre Trudeau is a shy man but a natural performer, a man with incredible personal style, engaging and abrasive, subdued and ebullient, accessible and cold and remote, and warm.

I tried painting Trudeau three times. The first was almost all white, with canvases stacked on top of each other. For some reason, I tried "stacking" Laurier as well, but that Trudeau was too papal. The second attempt was his early years, the flashy glory days. Well, glory days are glory days, gone, and so is that version of a man I admire. Internationally, he has given us stature we've never had.

I decided on the ten'-by-six' proportion to underscore Trudeau's presence, ten feet high. The image is marginally related to my 1958 painting, "The Visitor." It also had an enigmatic quality, a slightly threatening air. The Maltese Cross is obviously a form I like. It is used here because of Trudeau's religion. His Jesuit education had a strong bearing on his life. The intellectual discipline from Jean Brébeuf College is in his bones, but the halo-like cross is slipping a bit.

The painting has two sections; the division runs from upper right to bottom left. The right side is softer. Trudeau has a gentler side to him, seen when he is with his children. Trudeau is not finished yet, he will go on to play some part, perhaps internationally. I could still add one or two panels, panels in the mind, the future.

The other side is hard, rigid, disciplines, but not entirely so. Trudeau has too much heart to be totally hard-edged. He can be explosive. His life seems dominated by logic, but emotion bursts through. I have often used borders in my paintings, but here, for the first time, there is only half a border. It contains a blue reminiscent of the Quebec flag and gives that side of the painting, as an integral part of the whole, a more structures and firmer sense. The division is, in part, a device to make the painting work.

The stripes are entirely hard-edged and bold, like Trudeau's discipline, strength and authority. A huge head-shape floats above the field of stripes. Everything about Trudeau seems centered on his mind. The head dominates. The things that look like cogs are actually part of a construction drawing of the female form. The head-shape has its back turned to three-quarters profile. It is commanding, remote and removed. The black and grey — severe, powerful and even ominous colours — emphasize dominance and distance, while remaining enigmatic. The awkwardness is deliberate. I did not try to pretty it up. Trudeau has incredible eyes, brilliant and sharp like a fox's. He seems able to look through you. The eyes in the painting are like him, always seeing. The second set are akin to the mind's eye, the eye that imagines what is beyond the seen.

▲ Photo: William Ronald with former PM Pierre Trudeau at the opening of the exhibition *The Prime Ministers*, Art Gallery of Ontario, 1984

Index